ANCIENT GREEK
LITERARY LETTERS

What was it about epistolarity that appealed so strongly to the Greek imagination? The first reference in Greek literature to a letter occurs in our oldest extant Greek poem, Homer's *Iliad*. But letters can be found lurking in every corner of ancient Greek writing. This book aims to bring the literary letters themselves into clear view for contemporary readers.

Many ancient writers included letters in other narrative genres: Euripides brought letters on stage; historians included letters as documents; Greek novelists sprinkled their stories with letters exchanged between separated lovers; and epigrammatists played with the epigram as letter. By the second and third centuries CE, many centuries after Homer's epics, imaginative letters had evolved into an established genre in their own right: Aelian and Alciphron excelled in epistolary impersonations, imitating the voices of the lower classes, and collecting their letters in anthologies; Philostratus emerged as a master of epistolary spin, taking one theme and subtly tweaking it in half a dozen letters to different addressees; and anonymous writers competed with one another in their particular form of ghost-writing for the rich and famous.

Arranged chronologically, with introductory sections for each time period, this book studies a wide range of writers, genres and literary levels and suggests that there is more to a letter than just the information it communicates. Epistolary context is just as important as content, as will be rediscovered by Ovid, Richardson, Laclos, and a whole host of later European writers. Patricia A. Rosenmeyer has chosen a highly entertaining selection, which includes translation of previously inaccessible or untranslated works, and deftly opens up a neglected area of study to provide an enjoyable and significant survey for students of Greek epistolography.

Patricia A. Rosenmeyer is Professor of Classics at the University of Wisconsin-Madison.

ANCIENT GREEK LITERARY LETTERS

Selections in translation

Patricia A. Rosenmeyer

Routledge
Taylor & Francis Group

LONDON AND NEW YORK

First published 2006
by Routledge
2 Park Square, Milton Park, Abingdon, Oxon OX14 4RN

Simultaneously published in the USA and Canada
by Routledge
270 Madison Ave, New York, NY 10016

Routledge is an imprint of the Taylor & Francis Group

© 2006 Patricia A. Rosenmeyer

Typeset in Garamond 3 by
Florence Production Ltd, Stoodleigh, Devon
Printed and bound in Great Britain by
TJ International Ltd, Padstow, Cornwall

British Library Cataloguing in Publication Data
A catalogue record for this book is available from the British Library

Library of Congress Cataloging in Publication Data
A catalog record for this book has been requested

ISBN10: 0–415–28550–X (hbk)
ISBN10: 0–415–28551–8 (pbk)

ISBN13: 978–0-415–28550–6 (hbk)
ISBN13: 978–0-415–28551–3 (pbk)

CONTENTS

CONTENTS

ACKNOWLEDGMENTS

The original idea for this book came, most appropriately, in the form of a letter from Richard Stoneman; I have appreciated his encouragement and patience throughout the writing process. John Henderson supported this project from its earliest stages; his suggestions for improvement were gratefully received, as were those of the anonymous readers for the press. I have benefited from conversations with colleagues, students, and friends, including Kasia Hagemajer Allen, Philip Altman, William Aylward, Colleen Bayley, Kenneth Katz, Alexandra Pappas, Angela Pitts, Thomas Rosenmeyer, and Irene Ramalho Santos. Vasiliki Kostopoulou assisted with early drafts of several translations, and Patricia Hanson supplied wise counsel at critical moments. My research was made possible by a summer grant from the University of Wisconsin Graduate School Research Council, a Vilas Associates Award, and a sabbatical leave from the University of Wisconsin during the academic year 2004–2005.

I signed a contract for this book just after my daughter Sarah's first birthday; it will be in press as she begins to read and write. Her older brother Daniel already fully understands epistolary conventions, as well as the multiple uses to which letters may be put; his (deceptive) letter to the tooth fairy was a model of persuasive rhetoric, even if it eventually failed to convince. Although the pressures of raising a family while pursuing an academic career can be overwhelming at times, I have had wonderful role models at each stage of my professional life. As my dissertation advisor, Froma Zeitlin was inspirational, if inimitable; visits to her office or home were always intellectual feasts. As a mentor in my first academic position, Ruth Scodel showed me that combining motherhood and academic excellence was not only possible but also (deceptively) easy. As my first successful doctoral student, Marie Flaherty Jones taught me that, whatever larger life plans we may have, the children always think they come first. I am deeply grateful to these three women for all they have taught me, and for helping me find my own way.

Finally, this book could not have been completed without Marie Flaherty Jones, who has been its fairy godmother throughout. She read numerous drafts, livened up my prose, and sharpened fuzzy conclusions. I owe her an enormous debt of gratitude.

INTRODUCTION

In the sixth book of the *Iliad*, Homer recounts the story of
Bellerophon, a handsome young man of noble blood who visits King
Proteus in Argos. The king's wife Anteia falls in love with their guest
and tries to seduce him, but when Bellerophon refuses to play along,
she quickly turns the tables on him. Anteia announces to her
husband that the young man has assaulted her, and the king is forced
to take action. Unwilling to pollute his own hands with the murder
of a guest, Proteus sends Bellerophon away with a sealed message in
his hands to deliver to Anteia's father, the king of Lycia (*Il.* 6.
167–70):

> He rejected the idea of killing him, since he had an
>   honorable heart;
> instead he sent him to Lycia and gave him a grim message
>   to take along,
> writing down many things in the folded tablets, things
>   that would destroy a man's soul;
> he commanded Bellerophon to show them to Anteia's
>   father, plotting to have him killed.

These folded tablets with their fatal commands are the first step
in a series of delayed death sentences, as the king of Lycia is no
more eager to commit murder than Proteus had been. Bellerophon
fortunately survives Anteia's false accusation and the king's death
warrant. The tablets are presumably recycled, sent back later with
some more mundane message inscribed on their surfaces. On another
level, the epistolary part of the story is recycled in Shakespeare's
Hamlet, where the dramatist finds the idea of a dangerous sealed
letter in the unwitting protagonist's hands too enticing a plot device
to ignore.

1

This literary anecdote shows in a nutshell just how far back the epistolary impulse can be traced in the Greek imagination, and how influential it was for later Western literature. The first recorded example of an epistolary act—a reference to a folded tablet with written signs, whether alphabetic or pictographic—occurs in our earliest extant example of ancient Greek literature, and may have been part of an even older mythic tradition.

When we start consciously looking for them, letters can be found lurking in every corner of ancient Greek writing. But this book aims not only to bring the letters themselves into clear view for contemporary readers, but also to draw attention to what lies at the very heart of the various types of letters collected here, namely the epistolary impulse at work in Greek literature, the Greek epistolary imagination. We can set aside the question of whether letters are fictional or real, historical or literary—a highly problematic issue that has been addressed elsewhere (Trapp 2003; Rosenmeyer 2001; Luck 1961)—and focus instead on the writer's imagination, both his personal imagination and the large part of his imagination that is culturally determined and shared. Many writers chose to include letters in other narrative genres: Euripides brought letters on stage; historians included letters for their documentary cachet; Greek novelists sprinkled their stories with letters exchanged between separated lovers; and epigrammatists played with the idea of epigram as letter (paradoxical in that the purported origin of the epigram was an inscription on stone, surely one of the least portable of all ancient writing surfaces). By the second and third centuries CE, many centuries after Homer's epics were written down, imaginative letters evolved into an established genre in their own right: Aelian and Alciphron excelled in epistolary impersonations, imitating the voices of the lower classes; Philostratus emerged as a master of epistolary spin, taking one theme and subtly tweaking it in half a dozen letters to different addressees; and anonymous writers competed with one another in their particular form of ghostwriting for the rich and famous.

What was it about epistolarity that appealed so strongly to the Greek imagination? Why did so many authors repeatedly turn to epistolary narration, and to what effect? Let me offer one brief example to illustrate the nature of the question. When Euripides composed his tragedy *Hippolytus*, he was working from a traditional version of the story that did not include a letter: as in the Bellerophon passage above, an older married woman falls in love with a younger man, and upon being rejected by him, accuses him falsely of trying to seduce her, after which the innocent victim is unjustly punished. We know that Euripides produced two versions of the play during his lifetime; in the first version, Phaedra spoke of her desire directly to her stepson Hippolytus, in an onstage gesture that the Athenian audience objected to as going beyond the bounds of conventional female decorum. The play was not well received. According to the hypothesis (the ancient summary) of the second version, Euripides then rewrote his play in order to remove the morally offensive features of the first version (Barrett 1964: 10–45). He did this by killing Phaedra offstage before she could meet face-to-face with the object of her desire. But Euripides still had to find a way to communicate Phaedra's deceit to her husband Theseus.

A letter was the perfect solution. Letters make present the voice of a person who is absent. In this case, Phaedra is not just temporarily absent or physically separated from her interlocutor, but permanently silenced. Yet the written words, etched on a sealed tablet that dangles from her dead wrist, replace her living voice; by virtue of their textual nature, they have an even greater impact on Theseus than a spoken accusation would have (Calame 1993: 796–8; Segal 1992; Garrison 1989). When father and son finally meet, nothing Hippolytus can say in his defense will convince Theseus of his innocence. On the level of theatrical spectacle, the tablet serves as a vivid prop that must have attracted the audience's gaze immediately. Part of the tension of the scene is the suspense surrounding the letter as physical object. When will Theseus notice the piece of damning evidence? Will he read it out loud so that we, too, can hear Phaedra's words? When he finally does break the seal and read the letter to himself, it turns out to be both horrible and at some level wholly "unreadable" (*Hipp.* 875: *oude lekton*), but the audience does not really need to hear the precise words to understand Theseus' shock and the full horror of the situation. The dead Phaedra protects her reputation and gets her revenge through the letter, and Theseus condemns his son to a grisly death.

It is not too much of an exaggeration to say that the device of the letter turned Euripides' initial dramatic disaster into a success for the ages. But before we can explore the wider appeal of the letter as literary trope here, let us first consider the primary function of the letter. In his recent anthology of Greek and Latin letters, M. Trapp offers a useful basic definition (Trapp 2003: 1):

A letter is a written message from one person (or set of people) to another, requiring to be set down in a tangible medium, which itself is to be physically conveyed from sender(s) to recipient(s). Formally, it is a piece of writing that is overtly addressed from sender(s) to recipient(s), by the use at the beginning and end of one of a limited set of conventional formulae of salutation (or some allusive variation on them) which specify both parties to the transaction. One might also add, by way of further explanation, that the need for a letter as a medium of communication normally arises because the two parties are physically distant (separated) from each other, and so unable to communicate by unmediated voice or gesture; and that a letter is normally expected to be of relatively limited length.

Trapp's definition hits on many of the aspects emphasized by ancient epistolary theorists whose goal was to advise prospective letter writers how best to communicate their messages: be clear and concise; follow conventions of style and address; keep in mind the status and mood of your addressee; and be aware that your letter reflects your own personality (Malherbe 1988: 12–13). But alongside this primary function of a letter to communicate information there exists a parallel world of secondary functions and complications. More interesting than the information conveyed (the "what") are the ramifications of how, why, when, to whom, in spite of whom, and in place of what these letters are created and delivered. In most cases, epistolary context is just as important as content.

Looking back at the Euripidean example, one could say that the information contained in the letter, while false, is its most critical part; it certainly moves the dramatic action forward. But Euripides could easily have achieved the same thing through other means: through his original face-to-face encounter, through a "messenger" speech, through Phaedra's confessions to her nurse, or even through a direct confrontation between Phaedra and Theseus. But the presence of a letter in this scene hints at other important dimensions. Phaedra uses a letter because she prefers not to speak directly; she prefers indirection because she is lying, and thus can convince her addressee better in writing than in person, and because she is inherently respectable enough to be ashamed of her passion, preferring the distancing and controllable format of writing to the messy and emotional communicative act of spoken words. She retains control over her addressee's reaction by killing herself, thus forestalling any interruption or response that might cast doubt upon her motives and veracity.

There are two principal advantages to choosing a letter format over reported direct speech within non-epistolary genres. One is the assumption that we gain insight into the motivations and feelings of the players; the letter offers the illusion of a direct glimpse into the character's heart and mind. Thus the letter is particularly suited for erotic intrigue: the novelists embed letters in their narratives when separated lovers exchange secrets (*Chaereas and Callirhoe; Leucippe and Clitophon*) or young women express romantic feelings for their beloveds (*Apollonius King of Tyre*). One could compare the letter to a diary in that both offer a safe and contained environment for uncensored emotions; they differ, of course, in that the letter always assumes another person as an addressee. Other emotions are also well served by epistolary representation. When Euripides shows Agamemnon writing and erasing, sealing and unsealing, a letter to Clytemnestra in *Iphigenia in Aulis*, the audience can experience his agonies of indecision more vividly than through speech alone. And when the illiterate Iphigenia in *Iphigenia in Tauris* commissions a letter in the hope that someday, someone will come along to deliver it to Orestes, we understand better the depths of her enduring misery and desperation.

A second main advantage to letters is their association in the human mind with documentary proof. Just as material objects allow archaeologists to draw conclusions about aspects of antiquity, so letters can function as physical objects, documents that have managed to survive intact over years or even centuries. This, of course, works particularly well when the letter is written by hand and signed by its purported author, but in the case of most ancient literary examples, we are forced to accept other markers of authenticity, such as "and he wrote as follows." Thus, when Herodotus on occasion interrupts the flow of historical narrative in order to insert a letter from some king or general, we are automatically disposed to believe he is recording actual texts of actual letters; the author who includes letters in his work becomes an archivist, not just a good storyteller.

Later in the tradition, our inclination to trust authentic-sounding letters will be both tested and teased. The pseudonymous letters, for example, were certainly not historical documents. But their authors, who wrote in the voices of famous figures from the past, mixed in just enough historical information with their amusing invented scenarios to be convincing. They clearly found an eager audience for their historically informed imitations of great men's private correspondences. One can understand the desire to be privy to Socrates' or

Solon's innermost thoughts expressed on paper, a desire so basic to human nature that one could forgive a person for imagining these pseudonymous letters to be genuine; alternatively, these letters could have been appreciated as consummate examples of rhetorical skill, i.e. what Aeschines or Demosthenes might have written to their friends or family under specific circumstances and if given the opportunity to do so. So, too, the authors of the novellas *Chion of Heraclea* and the *Letters of Themistocles* must have been attracted to epistolary format because the fictional aspects of the correspondence could be integrated with solid historical knowledge, creating a more vivid and convincing historical fiction (or fictional history). Themistocles' letters offer insights into not just his own controversial roles in Athenian and Persian politics, but those of his contemporary Pausanias, as well. Chion's letters record his personal development and at the same time chart actual historical events as they are in the process of unfolding. For Greek readers, who historically had a strong aversion to any form of tyranny, there must have been a real temptation to accept as genuine these letters of an unformed young man who grew into a brave and daring tyrant slayer.

With the epistolary novella, we have shifted from embedded letters to free-standing epistolary collections. While a modern reader may easily accept letters inserted into non-epistolary narratives as effective literary devices, the concept of letters as a genre in their own right is slightly more difficult to understand. But in antiquity, epistolary form admits a huge range of generic and stylistic affiliations. Epigrammatists in the Hellenistic period wrote elegiac verse love letters (Rufinus), epistolary party invitations (Philodemus), and short letters accompanying gifts. An anacreontic poet of the same period composed a lyric ode to a dove in charge of transporting letters between the archaic poet Anacreon and his beloved boy Bathyllus (*Anacreontea*). In the period of the Second Sophistic, epistolarity came into its own golden age. Lucian used letters as an alternative to dialogue form (*Letters of Kronos*), the emperor Hadrian's freedman Phlegon transcribed a ghost story in the form of a letter (*A Ghost Story*), and the anonymous author of *Chion of Heraclea* composed an epistolary novella.

Perhaps the most interesting epistolary phenomenon at this time was the emergence of the *pseudonymoi*, anonymous authors writing in the voices of famous people. These authors approached their subjects as if they were experimenting with the rhetorical trope of *ethopoieia*, a kind of impersonation originating in school exercises in which the speaker tried to illuminate a figure from the past through a more

6

intimate character portrayal. Thus a well-known figure like Socrates is presented writing a letter or a series of letters to a friend or family member, revealing feelings, thoughts, ideas, and private experiences, all of which were carefully juxtaposed with enough historical and biographical data to make the text believable. The letter format allowed more stylistic freedom than other genres (e.g. collected sayings, treatises, official decrees) since these private letters were understood to have been composed for a friend's eyes only; their intrinsically ephemeral nature allowed their authors a great deal of artistic freedom, as long as they contained no obvious anachronisms or blatantly incorrect (from the perspective of the supposed "real" author) viewpoints. So many of these pseudonymous texts have survived from antiquity that we can safely assume an eager reading public. Just as we are happy to be enlightened and entertained by the publication of private letters by artistic or political prodigies, even if some collections turn out later to be forgeries, so ancient readers must have turned to these letters as supplements to more traditional ways of honoring famous (or infamous) men (e.g. funerary epitaphs, official "lives," etc.). Whether the authors intended to deceive, or whether ancient readers actually were deceived, are impossible questions to answer; but the appeal of reading someone else's personal mail is undeniable.

The final group of epistolary authors presented in this collection begins with the same impulse as the *pseudonymoi* but differs from them in two crucial details: first, they attach their own names to their work and make explicit the assumption of a literary persona; and second, they largely focus on the lives not of the rich and famous, but on the poor and obscure. Aelian and Alciphron use letters to imagine life on the other side of the tracks, writing in the voices of farmers, fishermen, parasites and prostitutes. They have more room to maneuver than their counterparts who select the heavy-weights of history as their subjects, because their people are wholly invented. Also, their sophisticated reading audience would most likely not have the knowledge (paradoxically) to argue with the literary depictions, unfamiliar as they were with the daily lives of their social inferiors. Of course these intimate glimpses into the lives of the common people are not really about them at all, but rather entertaining narratives tailored to the tastes of readers who can enjoy their own cultural superiority while slumming on paper. Why else would Aelian allow his farmers to write letters at all, much less in an Attic almost purer than Plato's? Why else would Alciphron slip in clever allusions to Homer, Sappho, Menander, and other favorite sophistic culture heroes? Here author and audience are clearly in collusion for the sake of literary entertainment, and epistolary form allows the entertainment to succeed.

The odd man out in this final group similarly takes on different personas, but in his case, all the personas are variations on himself: Philostratus postures at will, reinventing himself with every letter, trying on new lovers for size. He addresses anonymous beloveds, both male and female, and the sheer number of letters within the collection gives the impression of someone addicted to writing. His letters take on whatever tone he thinks will succeed in seducing the object of his desire: flattering, blaming, advising, threatening, or promising. His epistolary collection represents the logical out-come of a literary exercise where the point is not sincerity or seriousness, but rather rhetorical variation and artistic skill. We are invited to admire his many-sidedness, as he turns into the Odysseus of epistolarity in the campaign of *eros*. The letter is one of the only genres in which the writer can reinvent himself with every new page, as every act of letter writing is a process of self-creation and selective self-representation. Philostratus' unique contribution is to take away all our points of reference—his persona is constantly changing, his addressees are unnamed—and to leave us only with the pure and unelaborated epistolary impulse.

In the second chapter of my collection, I present a passage from the fourth-century BCE comic writer Antiphanes in which the main character, Sappho, poses a riddle about a female creature who carries in her arms babies who, although they are mute, can be heard across the ocean. When her companions admit they are stumped by her riddle, she provides the answer (Kassel and Austin 1983: fr.194):

> The female creature is a letter,
> and the babies she carries around inside are the letters
>   of the alphabet.
> Even though they have no voice, they chat with people
>   far away,
> whomever they desire. But if someone else happens
>   to stand
> near the person reading the letter, he won't hear a thing.

I think of my own selections in translation as a kind of open letter to readers who may not have encountered this material before, or who are suspicious of its nature. Antiphanes' passage implies that letters are powerful, secretive, and intended to compensate for absence: "if someone happens to stand near . . . he won't hear a thing." Just as a canvas of pointillism resembles nothing more than a collection of colorful dots when viewed close up, so, too, some of these fictional letters can seem shapeless and confusing (not to mention overwhelming) when read "close up" in their entirety. Thus, while I have included the novellas *Chion of Heraclea* and the *Letters of Themistocles* in their entirety (Chapter 4), I have ruthlessly pared down the selections from such prolific authors as the pseudonymous writers (Chapter 5) and the imperial epistolographers Alciphron and Philostratus (Chapter 6). But I have made every effort to provide the reader with a sampling that is sufficient for gaining a sense of what I have termed the ancient Greek epistolary imagination.

This collection is intended primarily for the general reader, and assumes no knowledge of ancient Greek. It is organized chronologically, with a brief introductory essay before each set of translations. But for those who wish to consult more specialized sources, I include below a brief overview of suggested further readings.

Suggested further reading

In the past decade there has been a surge of interest in fictional letters, as is evidenced by the following publications: N. Holzberg, *Der griechische Briefroman: Gattungstypologie und Textanalyse* (1994); C.D.N. Costa, ed., *Greek Fictional Letters: a Selection with Introduction, Translation and Commentary* (2001); P.A. Rosenmeyer, *Ancient Epistolary Fictions: the Letter in Greek Literature* (2001); and M. Trapp, ed., *Greek and Latin Letters: an Anthology with Translation* (2003). While both Costa and Trapp provide selections in Greek, the only complete collection of Greek epistolary texts in the original language remains that of R. Hercher, *Epistolographi graeci* (1873).

While I have not included examples from early Christian epistolography in this collection, the following volumes on the subject may be useful: W. Speyer, *Die literarische Fälschung im heidnischen und christlichen Altertum* (1971); J.L. White, *Light from Ancient Letters* (1986); S.K. Stowers, *Letter Writing in Greco-Roman Antiquity* (1986); and M.L. Stirewalt, Jr., *Studies In Ancient Greek Epistolography* (1993).

Finally, for those readers who crave a bit of theory with their texts, I offer an eclectic sampling of ancient and modern epistolary theory that has informed my own approach to the material: H. Koskenniemi, *Studien zur Idee und Phraseologie des griechischen Briefes bis 400 n. Chr.* (1956); G. Luck, "Brief und Epistel in der

Antike," *Das Altertum* 7 (1961) 77–84; K. Thraede, *Grundzüge griechisch-römischer Brieftopik* (1970); J. Lacan, "Seminar on the Purloined Letter," tr. J. Mehlman, *Yale French Studies* 48 (1972) 38–72; J. Derrida, *The Post Card: from Socrates to Freud and Beyond* trans. A. Bass (1987); J.G. Altman, *Epistolarity: Approaches to a Form* (1982); S. Kauffman, *Discourses of Desire: Gender, Genre, and Epistolary Fiction* (1986); A.J. Malherbe, *Ancient Epistolary Theorists* (1988); and E. Goldsmith, *Writing the Female Voice: Essays in Epistolary Literature* (1989).

1

CLASSICAL GREEK
LITERARY LETTERS

INTRODUCTION

This section of the anthology includes epistolary passages embedded in classical tragedy and history. In the fifth and early fourth centuries BCE, references to letters and the written word begin to crop up more frequently in literature, especially in the pages of historians and in performance on the Athenian stage. Aeschylus (*Prometheus Bound* 460–1) praised writing in general as a benefit to mankind and a mark of advanced civilization, while **Euripides** (*Palamedes* 578 Nauck) extolled the usefulness specifically of letters in keeping people informed about the affairs of friends and relatives abroad. Cratinus, an older contemporary of Aristophanes, included in one of his comedies a scene in which a letter was read out loud: at one point, an unidentified character says "now listen to this letter!" (Kassel and Austin 1983: 316). The historians **Herodotus, Thucydides,** and **Xenophon** focused on the power of written messages to communicate across enemy lines, as commanders sought ever more secure ways to send military secrets. While most of the passages below are fairly brief, they highlight themes that will recur in later post-classical epistolary narratives, namely urgent appeals for assistance in times of crisis, mistaken deliveries to the wrong addressee, dangerous misreadings, and scribbled confessions of secret passions.

Euripides (ca. 485–406 BCE) gave the letter serious attention in at least three of his plays, selections from which appear below. He used letters as one technique of many with which he could enliven the traditional narrative form of a tragic play. The letter itself was a visual prop that could vary the pacing of a scene, identify a courier by its seal, or deceive its recipient with a false message; when read out loud on stage, the contents of the letter could replace a stock messenger's speech, imparting information to the audience about

11

actions that could not otherwise easily be revealed. Like a camera zooming in for a close-up in the cinema, a letter could collapse the physical distance of the audience from the stage, as viewers were invited to read over the shoulder of the actor in a brief moment of epistolary intimacy.

In the first selection, from *Iphigenia in Tauris* (lines 727–87), Iphigenia has been living in exile for many years among the Taurians, hoping someday to return to her family in Argos. In the meantime, her duty as priestess of a local cult demands that she arrange for human sacrifices to satisfy Artemis. Two strangers—Orestes and Pylades—appear on her shores, and she decides to sacrifice one but spare the other to act as a messenger. As this scene begins, Iphigenia is about to hand over a letter addressed to her brother Orestes in Argos, and she expresses her anxiety about the reliability of her chosen messenger. She asks Pylades to swear an oath that he will complete the task, but Pylades wonders aloud what will happen if the letter is accidentally lost along the way. In response, Iphigenia recites its contents out loud, so that he can deliver the message with or without the actual tablet in his hands. Iphigenia herself is illiterate, and had previously dictated the letter to a slave. But she has long since memorized its contents, and views the letter as a kind of magic talisman, her only chance for communication with the civilized world she once knew. Euripides cleverly creates the opportunity for Iphigenia to recite the letter on stage; its contents, once made public, both remind the audience of Iphigenia's experiences after her apparent murder at Aulis, and also allow Orestes to recognize his long-lost sister. Her faith in the power of a letter is justified, and Pylades, far from having to worry about a long and dangerous sea voyage with the tablets in his possession, simply turns to his companion and places them in Orestes' hands. The scene ends with an emotional reunion, and the three successfully flee Tauris.

In *Iphigenia in Aulis* (lines 34–123), which was composed later than the previous play but covers an earlier part of the heroine's story, the Greek fleet is becalmed at the port of Aulis on its way to fight in Troy. The Greek leader Agamemnon is desperate to appease Artemis, who has stopped the favorable winds from blowing. When the Greeks consult their oracles, they are told to sacrifice Agamemnon's daughter Iphigenia or give up all hope of sailing to Troy. Confronted with an impossible situation, Agamemnon is forced to comply with the divinity's cruel request. Before this scene opens, he has written a letter inviting his wife and daughter to Aulis on the pretext of marrying Iphigenia to Achilles, but in reality intending to obey the oracle and kill her. In the passage below, as he seals and unseals a letter by lamplight, he admits to a trusted slave that he has made a terrible mistake, and has decided to write a new letter warning them not to come. He reads its contents out loud and urges his messenger to hurry, but his good intentions come too late; the revised message will be intercepted by Odysseus, and Clytemnestra and Iphigenia, obeying the first letter's instructions, have already landed on the shores of Aulis. The play ends with the apparent sacrifice of Iphigenia, although the ancient audience would certainly have known the alternative ending that Euripides had already staged in his *Iphigenia in Tauris*.

The final selection below is probably the most famous epistolary scene in Euripidean tragedy: the confrontation between Theseus and his dead wife Phaedra in *Hippolytus* (lines 856–80), which has already been discussed at some length. Here the author plays with and eventually disappoints our expectation that Theseus will read Phaedra's letter out loud on stage so that we, too, can learn its contents. Euripides first postpones the reading, teasing us as Theseus tries to imagine his wife's last words, and the tension mounts as we suspect the worst. In the end, Theseus is so horrified at the evil words within that he cannot bear to repeat what the tablet "screams out," namely her (false) accusation of rape at the hands of his son, Hippolytus. In this case, the letter remains a visual prop, its contents undisclosed, and our curiosity thus unsatisfied on one level. But we know the power of the deceitful message is enough for Theseus to condemn his son to a horrible death. Theseus privileges his dead wife's text over Hippolytus' spoken denials, but will be forgiven for his error on his son's deathbed.

Two passages from the fifth-century historian **Herodotus** follow. The first (3.40–3) claims to be a friendly letter of advice from Amasis, the pro-Greek pharaoh of Egypt in the latter part of the sixth century BCE, to Polycrates, the tyrant of Samos. This letter, it turns out, is what inspires Polycrates to throw away his famous emerald seal ring, which then re-emerges as a bad omen in the stomach of a fish served to him at dinner. Upon learning this, Amasis cuts off all correspondence, refusing to sustain friendly relations with a man so clearly destined to come to a bad end. The second passage (7.239) describes an elaborate method of sending a message in wartime: instead of writing on top of the thin wax coating of a wooden tablet, which allowed for constant melting and re-use, the exiled Spartan king Damaratus scraped all the wax off, wrote his message on the bare wood, and re-covered the tablet with a layer of smooth wax. This trick works almost too well: the Spartans who receive it are at first thoroughly confused. But eventually Gorgo, the wife of the Spartan leader Leonidas, sees through the ruse and suggests looking underneath the wax. Herodotus elsewhere in his *History* delights in narrating ever more complicated methods of keeping letters safe en route. One officer sews a letter in the belly of a hare and dresses his messenger up as a hunter (1.123). Another shaves the head of a slave, tattoos letters onto his skin, and waits until the hair grows back before sending the man out (5.35); the recipient merely has to shave the slave's head in order to read this "human" letter.

While we are not told how Herodotus came by Amasis' letter, which he quotes directly, **Thucydides** (ca. 460–400 BCE) is more cautious about the documentary nature of his epistolary sources. In an early section in his history (1.128–32), Thucydides records a letter exchange between the Persian king Xerxes and the Spartan general Pausanias, introducing it with the tag "as it became known later." This lets us know that Thucydides is using reputable sources, perhaps even consulting archives, and not freely inventing what might have been a likely scenario between the two historical figures, as Herodotus may have done above (based on "how they say it happened"). Although we are given just one set of letters, we are told that Xerxes and Pausanias continue to correspond over time, using a go-between for the sake of security, since Pausanias plans to betray Greece to the Persians. Finally Pausanias is caught by one of his own messengers, who opens the letter he is carrying and discovers doubly damning evidence: Pausanias' treason, and a postscript directing the reader to kill the bearer of the message upon his arrival in the Persian court, in an attempt to avoid the possibility of information leaking back to the Greeks.

The Persians reappear as letter writers in the final epistolary selection from the classical historians: a passage from **Xenophon**'s narrative of Cyrus' upbringing, the *Education of Cyrus* (4.5.26–34). Xenophon's letter is true to formal epistolary conventions of opening and closing salutation ("Cyrus to Cyaxares, greetings" . . . "Farewell"). As with the two dramatic scenes in Euripides, we witness the sender reading his letter aloud to the messenger so that he can "understand and confirm the contents" if he is questioned. The contents of Cyrus' letters reflect both the friendly type of advice letter encountered above in Herodotus, and the military negotiations exemplified by Thucydides' exchanges between allies.

The epistolary passages introduced in this first chapter are all embedded in non-epistolary narratives; we will see later in the

Hellenistic and imperial periods how letters can emerge from their frames and stand independently. These classical letters contain elements of danger, treachery, and secret love, all of which appeared in Homer's reference to Bellerophon's "letter," and will reappear in many subsequent examples. With the exception of Phaedra's deceitful letter, all the passages from the classical period demonstrate the primary function of a letter, which is to convey information from one person in one place to another person in another place. But Phaedra's letter is an example of how else a letter can be used, namely by those who prefer not to speak directly to their audience, whether because they wish to conceal the fact that they are lying, or because they know that what they have to say will be more believable if it is in writing. Thus Phaedra's letter emphasizes the rhetorical nature of the epistolary form itself. Euripides' acknowledgment of the rhetorical power intrinsic in letter writing is an important milestone in Greek literary history.

CLASSICAL GREEK LITERARY LETTERS: THE TEXTS

Euripides

"Iphigenia in Tauris" 727–36, 753–87

IPHIGENIA   Here are the tablets, strangers, folded and written on many sides.
But there's something else I want.
People act differently when they face trouble;
they lose courage and become fearful.
I'm afraid that the person carrying my letter to Argos
will ignore my instructions
after he leaves this land.

ORESTES   What do you want then? What can I say
to convince you that you don't need to worry?

IPH.   Let him promise me that he'll carry this letter
to Argos, to my family . . .

PYLADES   But wait, here's a problem we've overlooked.

IPH.   Let's all hear it, if it's really important.

PYL.   Allow me this loophole: if something happens

15

to the ship, and the letter, along with the cargo, disappears
in the waves, and I manage to save only myself,
then the oath should no longer be binding.

IPH.   Well then, here's what I propose, since precautions
        are wise.
I'll tell you everything that's written in the folds of the letter,
so you can report it to my family.
Then all will be safe. If you save the tablet,
it will communicate in silence what's written on it.
But if this tablet is lost at sea,
by saving yourself, you'll save my message.

PYL.   I like your idea; it works for both of us.
So tell me who should receive this letter in Argos,
and what message I should pass on from you.

IPH.   Take this message to Orestes, Agamemnon's son . . .

PYL.   Oh my gods!

IPH.   Why are you calling on the gods as I speak?

PYL.   It's nothing, go on. I was thinking of something else.

IPH.   Orestes (I'm repeating the name so you won't forget it).
"These are the words of Iphigenia, who was sacrificed at Aulis
but is still alive, even though there there they think she's dead . . ."

OR.   Where is she? Has she come back from the dead?

IPH.   She's right in front of your eyes; stop interrupting me!
"Bring me back to Argos, brother, before you die,
and take me away from this barbarian land, away from the
        goddess'
awful sacrifices, where my duty is to kill foreigners . . ."

OR.   Pylades, what should I say? Where on earth are we?

IPH.   "or I'll become a curse upon your house."
Orestes might question you and doubt your story.
So tell him that the goddess Artemis saved me,
exchanging me for a deer, and that's what my father sacrificed,
thinking he was stabbing his sharp sword into my body.
She's the one who brought me to this country. This is my
        message,
and this is what's written on the tablets.

16

"Iphigenia in Aulis" 34–42, 89–91, 97–123

OLD MAN   . . . but you've lit the lamp
and are writing a letter, the one you have in your hand.
You erase the words you've already written,
seal it and then unseal it again,
and then you throw the wooden tablet on the ground,
weeping warm tears; in your confusion,
you almost seem to have gone mad.
What's bothering you? What disaster has struck, my king?

AGAMEMNON   . . . Calchas the prophet predicted that I would
have to sacrifice Iphigenia to Artemis . . .
Then my brother, using all sorts of arguments,
persuaded me to dare the worst. I wrote in the folds of a tablet
and sent it to my wife, telling her that
she should send our daughter here to marry Achilles . . .
That's how I convinced her, by inventing
a lie about the girl's wedding . . .
That was a bad decision, and I'm changing my mind
for the better now in this letter, the one you saw me
unsealing and sealing again tonight, old man.
So come and take this letter to Argos.
I'm going to tell you all that's written
in the folds of this tablet,
since you are loyal to my wife and my whole household.

OLD MAN   Yes, tell me, explain it to me, so that my words
will agree with your writing.

AGAM.   "I'm sending you another letter,
Clytemnestra, daughter of Leda,
ordering you not to send our daughter Iphigenia
to Aulis, its bay protected from waves
and jutting out toward Euboea.
We will plan the wedding party
for our child some other time."

"Hippolytus" 856–65, 874–80

THESEUS   Look, what's this, a tablet hanging from her own dear
hand?
Does it want to tell me some news?
Maybe my poor wife wrote me a message,

a last request about our marriage and our children?
Don't worry, poor thing. No other woman will
come into Theseus' home or his bed.
Now the image of her gold-carved seal ring
smiles up at me, the property of a dead woman.
I'll open the sealed cover
and see what this tablet wants to tell me . . .
Oh no, another evil on top of this evil,
I can't bear it, can't speak of it. Wretched me!

CHORUS   What? Tell me, if you can.

THESEUS   The tablet screams out, screams horrible things.
Where can I go to escape this weight of evils?
I'm completely destroyed by this song,
such a song I've seen, wretched me, calling out
in the writing.

Herodotus

3.40–3

Now Amasis noticed Polycrates' amazing good fortune, and was very concerned. When his fortune grew even greater, Amasis wrote a letter and sent it to Samos:

> Amasis writes to Polycrates as follows. It's wonderful to hear that a good friend and ally is doing well. But actually your great good fortune doesn't please me, because I know how jealous the gods can be. What I want for myself and my friends is a blend of good and bad fortune, a life spent sometimes succeeding and at other times failing, rather than doing well in everything. Because I've never heard of any man who did well all his life and then at the end didn't finish up horribly destroyed. So, if you trust my advice, do this to counteract your successes: think about what possession you value most, the one it would hurt the most to lose, and then throw it away so that no one will ever see it again. If from then on your successes are tempered by calamities, make sure you deal with it in the way I suggested.

Polycrates read the letter and realized that Amasis' advice was good, so he started looking through his treasures for one that it would break his heart to lose, and after searching for a while he found it: the seal ring he wore, with an emerald jewel set in gold, the work of Theodorus, son of Telecles, from Samos. He decided to throw it away and immediately took action. He put a crew on a fifty-oared ship, got on himself, and ordered them to put out to sea. When he was far away from his island, he took off the seal ring in full sight of the crew, and threw it into the water. After doing that, he sailed back and went into his house, thus having experienced misfortune.

But five or six days afterwards, the following occurred: a fisherman, catching a great big beautiful fish, decided to give it as a gift to Polycrates. He brought it to the door and asked to see Polycrates, and when he was in his presence, he handed over the fish and said, "My king, even though I make my living by fishing, when I caught this fish I decided not to sell it in the market; it's worthy of you and your greatness, so I'm bringing it to you as a gift." Polycrates was delighted by his little speech and answered in kind: "You've done the right thing, and I thank you twice—first for the gift, and second for your speech. Come and have dinner with me later." The fisherman was delighted with the invitation, and went home. But when the slaves cleaned the fish they found Polycrates' seal ring in its stomach. As soon as they saw it, they picked it up and carried it triumphantly to Polycrates; they gave him the ring and told him how they'd found it. When Polycrates saw that the gods had a hand in the matter, he wrote a letter and sent it off to Egypt, explaining all that he had done and what had happened.

Amasis read Polycrates' letter and realized that no man could save another man from his fate; Polycrates, who was so fortunate that he found even what he had thrown away, would not live happily ever after. So Amasis sent a messenger to Samos to say that he was dissolving their friendship. He did this because he knew that a terrible, overwhelming disaster would overtake Polycrates, and he didn't want to grieve in his heart for a friend.

7.239

When Xerxes made up his mind to lead his army against Greece, Demaratus, who was in Susa and was aware of the situation, wanted to send a message to the Spartans. But he was worried that he might be captured, so he had no way of communicating with them other than by this trick: he took a folded tablet, scraped the layer of wax off, and then wrote the king's plan on the surface of the wood. When he'd finished, he melted the wax and spread it back over the writing, so that the person carrying the blank tablet wouldn't be harassed by the guards on the way. When the tablet was taken to Sparta, the Spartans couldn't understand it until, so I'm told, Gorgo, who was Cleomenes' daughter and Leonidas' wife, figured it out by herself. She told them that if they scraped away the wax, they would find writing on the wooden surface underneath. They followed her suggestion, found the message, read it through, and then sent it on to the other Greeks. This is how they say it happened.

Thucydides

1.128–30, 132

Pausanias gave Gongylus a letter for Xerxes, which contained the following message, as it became known later:

> Pausanias, the general of Sparta, eager to do you a favor, returns these prisoners of war to you. I also intend, with your approval, to marry your daughter, and to put Sparta and the rest of Greece under your control. I think I can do this, with your help. So if any of this appeals to you, send someone we can trust to the coast so we can use him for our future correspondence.

This was all that was revealed in the writing.

Xerxes was delighted by the letter, and sent Artabazus, son of Pharnaces, to the coast, ordering him to replace Megabates, the previous governor in the satrapy of Dascylium. He also gave him a letter to take back to Pausanias in Byzantium, telling him to deliver it as quickly as possible, to show Pausanias the seal, and to perform quickly and discreetly any tasks that Pausanias might request of him related to the king's business. Artabazus arrived, did all the things he'd been told, and handed over the letter. The king had replied as follows:

> King Xerxes speaks thus to Pausanias. Because of the men you saved for me from Byzantium across the sea, you can count on my goodwill, stored up in my house and marked

down for eternity; I'm also pleased with your message. Let neither night nor day hold you back from keeping any of your promises to me, and let me know if you need any more supplies, whether gold, silver, or reinforcements of troops. You can count on Artabazus, a good man whom I've sent to you, to transact our business properly so that it works out best and most honorably for both of us.

After receiving this letter, although he was already highly esteemed by the Greeks as the hero of Plataea, Pausanias became prouder than ever, unwilling to live in the usual style; instead he dressed in Persian clothes when he left Byzantium and traveled through Thrace with a bodyguard of Persians and Egyptians.

Finally, so they say, the person who was going to give Artabazus Pausanias' last letter for the king, a man from Argilus who used to be Pausanias' favorite and was very loyal to him, turned informer. He was worried because none of the other messengers before him had ever returned; he made a copy of the seal, so that he wouldn't be exposed if his suspicions turned out to be false, or if Pausanias asked to rewrite some part of the letter. Then he opened the letter and found the postscript that he had suspected, namely an order to put him to death.

Xenophon

"Education of Cyrus" 4.5.26–34

The messenger was all set to depart for Persia . . . and Cyrus [king of the Persians] ordered him to take a letter to Cyaxares [king of the Medes]. Cyrus said "I also want to read the message aloud to you, so you can understand and confirm the contents, if Cyaxares asks you any questions about it." And this is what was in the letter:

> Greetings from Cyrus to Cyaxares. We haven't abandoned you; nobody is abandoned by his friends when he conquers his enemies. Nor do we think we've exposed you to danger by going away; in fact the reverse is true: the farther away we go, the more protection we provide for you. It's not the ones who stick closest to their friends who protect them best, but rather those who drive the enemy farthest away— they're the ones who best keep their friends out of danger. Think about how I've acted toward you, how you've acted

21

toward me, and how you still blame me for my behavior. Yet I've brought you allies, not just those you persuaded to come, but as many as I was able to bring; when I was in friendly territory, you gave me as many as I could persuade, but now that I'm in hostile lands, you call back not just those who don't want to stay, but all my men. So then I used to think that I owed you and your men a favor; but now you're forcing me to ignore you and to show all my gratitude to those men who've followed me. But I can't treat you the way you're treating me, so I'm sending a request to Persia for reinforcements; whoever comes to serve me will also be required to obey you, if you need them for anything before we return, and they should follow your wishes, not their own. In addition, even though I'm younger than you are, let me give you some advice: don't ask for something back once you've given it—you'll earn resentment instead of thanks; don't use threats if you want someone to come quickly; and don't threaten large groups of people while at the same time claiming you've been abandoned, because you'll just encourage people to ignore you. But we'll try to come as soon as we've finished doing the things we think will benefit both of us. Farewell.

Then Cyrus said to his messenger, "Deliver this letter to Cyaxares, and if he asks you anything about it, answer him in a way that agrees with what's written here. And I've told you all about the Persians just as it's written in the letter."

2

HELLENISTIC
LITERARY LETTERS

INTRODUCTION

In the late fourth and the third centuries BCE, official letter writing was an important way in which government officials maintained a presence in the expanding Hellenistic kingdoms in Egypt and Asia Minor. We have substantial remains of official, personal, and business correspondence from Ptolemaic Egypt, including letters on taxation, the sale of goatskins, over-pricing of olive oil, legal arguments in court, and private family feuds (Harris 1989: 128). But as far as we can tell from the extant evidence, letters did not appear with any greater frequency in Hellenistic literature than they had in the classical period. So although the literate public had acquired the epistolary habit in everyday life, the letter as literary device seemed to hold no particular attraction for writers of this period.

This conclusion must, of course, be tempered by an awareness of what we may be missing. A great deal of New Comedy is lost to us. The Hellenistic dramatists Alexis, Euthycles, and Machon all wrote comedies, now lost, with the title *Epistole*; their colleague Timocles staged an *Epistolai*. References to letters appear in three of Menander's plays—*Epitrepontes*, *Misoumenos*, and *Sicyonios*—possibly inspiring the Roman comic writer Plautus to open his play *Pseudolus* with an elaborate critique of a letter written on a wax tablet by a young man's girlfriend; the discussion between the unhappy lover and his slave, who reads the letter out loud on stage, includes snide comments on the girl's sloppy handwriting and bad spelling.

The evidence we do have of letters in Hellenistic literature is skimpy. In Herodas' verse *Mimes* (1.23–5), a woman complains that she hasn't received any letters in the last ten months from her absent partner, who is some sort of traveling salesman. In prose, the early second-century BCE historian Polybius writes of epistolary forgeries and the abuse of authority in the context of military campaigns (5.43.5–6; 5.50.11–12; 5.57.5; 5.61.3), much in the style of his classical predecessors. But letters play almost no part in the more canonical works of the three great third-century Alexandrian poets Callimachus, Theocritus, and Apollonius of Rhodes.

The Hellenistic selections below are from drama, epigram, and lyric poetry. **Antiphanes'** comedy *Sappho* comes from the fourth century BCE, and survives only in fragments. We know that Antiphanes, as a practitioner of Middle Comedy (after Aristophanes and before Menander), was both prolific and successful on stage in Athens, but we rely mostly on citations in the prose compiler Athenaeus (ca. 200 CE) for our extant passages. I chose this bit not for its outward form, since it is not actually epistolary in shape at all, but for its content. The comic character Sappho, presumably based on the archaic lyric poet, presents a riddle: what is female and holds close to her body babies who are mute but can be heard far away? Her male respondents suggest as an answer to her riddle the argumentative and greedy orators who have cowed the *demos* into silent submission. But Sappho reveals that the babies represent the written word, enveloped in a letter, which is gendered feminine in Greek; epistolary text is thus both stronger and stranger than any masculine civic rhetorical performance.

The remaining passages are shorter lyrics: the first two selections are from the *Greek Anthology* (= *AP*), and the last is an anacreontic poem preserved in an appendix to the same. **Rufinus**, whose date is uncertain, but who contributed thirty-six erotic epigrams to book five of the *Anthology*, composed one of his pieces (5.9) as a love letter, supposedly sent from Ephesus to his girlfriend Elpis back home. He includes both their names in the first line of greeting in conventional epistolary manner ("Rufinus to Elpis, greetings"), and puns on the verb of address, which has a double meaning: Rufinus sends "greetings" (*chairein*) but wonders if Elpis can "be happy" (*chairein*) without him. The poem ends with a form of the epistolary closing formula of farewell (*errosthai*), as the lonely lover realizes his only hope is to return to his beloved as swiftly as his letter-poem "flies to [her] eyes."

The second epigram, collected in book eleven of the *Greek Anthology*, is attributed to **Philodemus**, a philosopher and poet active in the first century BCE in Rome. While we have some twenty-five of his love poems preserved in the manuscripts, this piece is not erotic, but rather an epistolary invitation to his close friend, the Roman aristocrat Piso, to attend a party in honor of the philosopher

Epicurus' birthday. Philodemus leaves his name unstated, leading us to assume that Piso would immediately recognize the allusion to "your friend" in the text; or do we have enough creative vision to remove the poem from its anthology and imagine it in Philodemus' own familiar handwriting? In keeping with Epicurus' philosophical views, the feast will focus more on spiritual and intellectual fodder than on delicacies or expensive wines, and Philodemus seems fairly certain that this will be more than enough to attract his politically powerful friend.

My final choice is from an anonymous collection of short poems, mainly hedonistic in theme, based on the corpus of the archaic lyric poet Anacreon. The **anacreontics**, as they are called, celebrate love, wine, and song in a series of sixty poems in simple lyric meters dated to the late Hellenistic and early Roman periods. This poem is remarkable for the picture it gives us of a love letter in the process of being delivered by a dove or carrier pigeon. The narrator, speaking on our behalf, asks the dove what she is up to, and when the dove teases him with "you should see these letters I'm carrying" (15.9), we wonder if Anacreon's secret message to his beloved Bathyllus will be intercepted and opened. But the dove manages to stop herself from telling the narrator everything, and we are ordered to "be off" (15.19) so she can find the proper addressee and deliver her letter safely. We are left doubly disappointed: we get neither gossip for the tabloids about Anacreon's latest beloved, nor a glimpse of an unknown poem of the master of love himself, assuming that Anacreon would, of course, send a letter in verse. Such disappointment aptly mirrors our general regret that so few literary letters remain from the Hellenistic period.

The Hellenistic selections below reflect both their classical forebears and look forward to new directions in epistolarity. Antiphanes and the anacreontic poet may have been inspired by Euripides' earlier use of letters in his tragedies, while the selections from the *Greek Anthology* reveal an interest in free-standing letters that will become fully developed only in the Second Sophistic. The epigrammatic letters are both literary and at the same time fully functional letters. We can imagine Piso and Elpis smiling at the conceit of a letter in verse and saving the letter poems for frequent re-reading; or we can assume that the poets invented the occasion for the sake of their art, and wrote their texts for posterity, not for the named addressee. More importantly, however, is the fact that what may have begun as an occasional piece was then valued enough to be saved, collected, and eventually anthologized.

HELLENISTIC LITERARY LETTERS: THE TEXTS

Antiphanes

"Sappho" (Kassel and Austin (1983) fr. 194 = Athen. Deipn. 10.450e–1b)

In his play *Sappho*, Antiphanes presents the poet Sappho asking riddles in this way, while someone answers her, as follows.

So Sappho says:

There's a female creature who keeps her babies tucked safely in
    her arms,
and even though they have no voice, they send out a loud cry
over the sea waves and across the whole continent,
reaching whomever they wish, and even those who aren't present
can hear. But the babies themselves are mute.

And someone [an old man?] answers her:

The female creature you describe is the city,
and the babies she nurtures are the orators.
The loud cries of these men
bring in profit here across the sea from Asia and Thrace.
The citizens, deaf and dumb, sit near them
while they pontificate and constantly argue.

SAPPHO You've got it all wrong; how could an orator
be voiceless, old man?

OLD MAN If he's caught breaking the law three times.
But I thought I really understood
what you were talking about. So go on, tell me.

Then Antiphanes presents Sappho solving the riddle herself:

The female creature is a letter,
and the babies she carries around inside are the letters of the
    alphabet.
Even though they have no voice, they chat with people far away,
whomever they wish. But if someone else happens to stand near
the person reading the letter, he won't hear a thing.

"The Greek Anthology"

Rufinus

AP 5.9

I, Rufinus, send cheerful greetings to my sweetest Elpis,
if she can be cheerful when I'm not there.
I swear an oath on your eyes that I can't bear it anymore,
this loneliness, the separation, my solitary bed.
When I visit Coressus' hill and great Artemis' shrine,
I'm always dripping with tears.
But tomorrow I'm coming home. I'll fly to your eyes,
calling down a thousand blessings on you.

Philodemus

AP 11.44

Dear Piso, your friend who is loved by the Muses,
who honors Epicurus' birthday every year on the twentieth
day,
invites you to his humble home tomorrow, after the ninth
hour strikes.
You won't be served delicacies and cups of Chian wine,
but you'll see honest friends and hear better stories than the
ones told on Phaeacia.
And if you ever look kindly upon me, Piso,
we'll celebrate the twentieth in high style.

"Anacreontea"

Anacr. 15

Where, pretty dove, tell me where are you flying from?
Why do you rush through the air,
sprinkling and wafting out so much perfume?
Who are you? What are doing?
"Anacreon sent me to his boyfriend, Bathyllus,
lord and master of all right now.
Aphrodite sold me to Anacreon for a small song,
so I serve him in such ways.
You should see these letters I'm carrying for him today.
And he says he'll set me free very soon.

But even if he does, I'll stay by his side as a slave.
What's the point of flying over hills and fields,
scratching for wild seeds, and perching on trees?
Now I feast on bread nibbled from Anacreon's own hands.
He gives me wine to drink and toast with.
After drinking, I start to dance,
and when my master plucks his lyre, I shade him with
    my wings.
When he falls asleep, I doze on top of his lyre.
Now you have it all—be off!
You've made me more talkative than a crow, my friend."

3

LETTERS AND PROSE FICTIONS OF THE SECOND SOPHISTIC

INTRODUCTION

Greek writers of the second and third centuries CE enjoyed a political climate that nurtured a strong sense of Hellenic identity. Athens had long ago become a cultural backwater, and Rome had conquered the Greek-speaking world, but Roman emperors from Hadrian to Marcus Aurelius generally supported Greek literature and the arts. An allegiance to Greek culture, specifically the culture of classical Athens, was one way in which the educated elite of the empire could define themselves; this period became known as the Second Sophistic because of its creative re-use of fourth-century Athenian cultural and literary models, when the first sophists reigned supreme. Thus many of the literary products of this period are written in an erudite, allusive style, for a readership steeped in the classics and alert to evocations of classical precedents. By imitating past masters, authors invited their equally sophisticated readers to join in the "affirmation of a common heritage" (Jones 1986: 159). This is, of course, a very simplistic summary of a complex cultural phenomenon, but the interested reader can find further information in my bibliography (e.g. Whitmarsh 2001, Goldhill 2001, Schmitz 1997, Swain 1996, Dihle 1994, Anderson 1993, Jones 1986).

The popularity of the literary letter in this period can be traced back to its roots in the schoolroom (Kennedy 2003). Students learned prose composition and practiced oral presentation through specific written exercises (*progymnasmata*) that required them to produce concise but compelling character portraits of either well-known heroes or stock personality types. Further along in rhetorical training, more advanced compositions were produced as entertainment for an adult audience, in which the challenge was to display the greatest amount of wit and learning in the smallest compass. The idea of the fictional letter may have evolved from rhetorical exercises in which a character is placed in a specific situation; the characters and incidents could be fictitious or historical. This kind of characterization (*ethopoieia*) often took the form of "what would so-and-so say if . . . ?" (Russell 1983: 1–39). In the resulting rhetorical display, sometimes the speaker focused primarily on the character—"what did the farmer say on seeing a ship for the first time?"—and at other times on the emotions—"what did Achilles say over the corpse of Patroclus?" (Anderson 1993: 52). The authors of this period transferred favorite themes and devices from epideictic rhetoric to the written page. Some continued to embed their letters in other narrative forms, as their classical forebears had done; we will read examples of this approach in the chapter below. Others, like the anonymous author of *Chion of Heraclea*, removed the narrative frame and wrote a series of connected letters that could be read as a novella; and yet others chose to write collections of single letters in the voices of other people, whether historical ("Plato") or invented ("an Athenian farmer"). This flowering of epistolary creativity fits well into a period that paradoxically valued both the classics and novelty for its own sake.

The passages below come from prose fictional genres. Three of the authors are considered "novelists," while the other two are difficult to categorize generically. The most familiar name to most readers will be that of **Lucian** of Samosata—a town in Roman-ruled Syria—active in the mid-second century CE, who was a prolific author of primarily satirical prose. He did not limit himself to a single genre, but produced dialogues, novellas, rhetorical introductions (*prolalia*) and showy rhetorical speeches (*epideixis*). He also enjoyed the literary effect of the letter form, with an epistolary essay ostensibly addressed to his friend Philo entitled *How To Write History*, for example, and an epistolary preface to his dialogue *Nigrinus*. The first excerpt below comes from his most famous work, *A True Story*, a picaresque prose fiction written in the first person, which describes his adventures at the edge of the civilized world. At the point where this passage picks up, he is visiting Odysseus and Penelope on the Isle of the Blessed; just before he sails, Odysseus asks him to deliver a letter to his girlfriend Calypso on Ogygia, where the immortal nymph still pines for her lost epic hero. Lucian (the narrator) surreptitiously opens and reads the letter before landing on Calypso's island, just to make sure that Odysseus is not up to any of his old tricks that might endanger him and his crew, and exhibiting, as he does so, a healthy suspicion of letters and their occasionally fatal function in literature. Lucian (the author) has read his Homer well, and recalls in this scene Bellerophon's narrow escape in the *Iliad*. But the suspicion of epistolary abuse is unwarranted; instead, Odysseus' letter is both a love letter to Calypso and a letter of recommendation for the courier. The whole passage is also a sequel to the *Odyssey*, expanding on what was famously hinted at by Teiresias' prophecy in the Homeric epic.

The second selection is from Lucian's *Letters of Kronos*. Here Lucian imagines a letter exchange between representatives of two social groups—the poor and the rich—as they petition Kronos, demanding better treatment from their fellow men. The entire exchange consists of four letters: two from Kronos, and one each from the plaintiffs. I have selected two letters: one from Kronos to the rich, and the other the rich men's response, which both contain numerous allusions to the poor men's complaints and give a clearer picture of the whole problem. Although Kronos tries initially to pass on the responsibility for the situation to Zeus, the current Olympian ruler, he does take their complaints seriously, and tries to suggest some practical solutions. The letters' humor comes from cynical observations on human selfishness and petty cruelty, as well as from Kronos' resemblance less to the thundering deity we might expect than to a bureaucrat forced to combine the roles of legal arbitrator and frustrated social worker.

While Lucian's satires, quite influential for later European authors, are still familiar to many readers, the next author in this anthology is obscure even to most classicists. **Phlegon** was a Greek-speaking freedman from Tralleis in Asia Minor, writing at the time of the emperor Hadrian in the early second century CE (Hansen 1996). He wrote, among other works, the *Book of Marvels*, a compilation of thirty-five barely credible odd events. This peculiar genre, labeled "paradoxography" by nineteenth-century German scholars (Westermann 1839), can be considered an ancient predecessor of today's supermarket tabloids (Hansen 1996: 12–15). The collection is certainly entertaining in its sensationalism. Our selection is a ghost story retold in a letter, presumably sent by an eyewitness to a curious friend. The story survives at the beginning of a single damaged manuscript, with the result that the letter begins in the middle of a sentence; we may posit an initial epistolary greeting, since the letter follows closing conventions at the end. But the outline of the story is clear enough, as we meet a young girl Philinnion, who returns from the dead to spend several nights in the company of a man who is visiting her parents' house. The passage begins with her nurse's discovery of the two lovers in bed, and ends with the ghost's return to the grave and her traumatized lover's suicide.

The letters embedded in the Greek novels offer equally lurid and emotionally charged scenes. These novels are notoriously difficult to date precisely, but for current purposes we can place them between the first and third centuries CE (Reardon 1989: 5). The three passages selected below, from **Chariton**, **Achilles Tatius**, and the anonymous author of *Apollonius King of Tyre*, all share the same popular slant as Phlegon's work: they are pleasure reading, like a modern paperback tucked into a beach bag, although the well-educated could certainly find much in them to challenge their intellects. Embedded letters in the novels, much as they were in Athenian tragedy, are devices employed to vary the narrative rhythm, impart crucial information, and heighten tension as the plot unfolds. They give us the illusion of direct glimpses into the characters' hearts and minds, but are, of course, just as manufactured as what frames them.

In the first two selections, letters reunite separated lovers whose lives have been complicated by abductions, false deaths, or love triangles, so popular in the ancient novels. In **Chariton**'s novel, *Chaereas and Callirhoe*, Chaereas' pregnant wife Callirhoe, thinking Chaereas dead, marries Dionysius, the richest man in Miletus. Halfway through the story, Chaereas finally tracks her down and writes a letter begging her to return, but his letter is intercepted and read by none other than Dionysius himself. After many plot twists, during which almost every man who meets Callirhoe, including Artaxerxes the king of Persia, falls madly in love with her and tries to win her for himself, the couple are finally reunited. The novel ends with two further embedded letters: an official one from Chaereas to the king of Persia, announcing the return of his queen who had been captured in battle, and a private one from Callirhoe to Dionysius, entrusting her son to his care. Although we are told she sends it without Chaereas' knowledge, leaving open the possibility that she still loves Dionysius, her opening salutation says it all, as she addresses him as "her benefactor," no longer her husband. But even her carefully chosen words do not convince Dionysius that she willingly abandoned him, and he (mis)interprets her letter as a promise of "spiritual fidelity," and the presence of "their" son (whose father is really Chaereas) as an eternal bond between them.

While Chariton's novel is already halfway over before the first embedded letter appears, **Achilles Tatius** begins his novel *Leucippe and Clitophon* with a short letter (not included below) that sets the plot in motion by introducing the heroine Leucippe, who has been evacuated from her home in war-torn Byzantium and comes to stay with her cousin Clitophon's family in Tyre. The two fall in love and elope together, but they then fall victim to pirates, who pretend to decapitate Leucippe in full view of her new husband. Clitophon despairs, and then reluctantly agrees to marry a rich widow named Melite, but fate would have it that Leucippe has actually been sold as a slave on Melite's own estate. The passage below shows Leucippe's reproachful letter to Clitophon; she fills him in on what she's been through since they were separated, and faults him for his infidelity. As in the case of Callirhoe's letter above, Leucippe chooses her opening words very carefully: "to my master Clitophon . . . since you are my mistress' husband now." Clitophon quickly writes back to convince her of his loyalty, cleverly wording his salutation to put to rest her fear that his feelings for her have subsided: "greetings to my mistress, Leucippe." His first words to her rehearse, almost pedantically to our ears, the useful and comforting basic function of letter writing: "the letter shows you present even though you're still absent from me" (Koskenniemi 1956: 183–4). Eventually, to no reader's surprise, the lovers find their way back to one another.

Our final selection, from the anonymous story entitled *Apollonius King of Tyre*, offers a sincere variation on Phaedra's deceitful letter discussed earlier. Here, a young girl turns to writing on a wax tablet as a way of expressing the true erotic feelings she is too modest to reveal otherwise; as she says, "the wax has no sense of shame." The eponymous hero of the tale, Apollonius, recently shipwrecked and destitute, is hired to tutor the daughter of the king who rescued him. She is being courted by several eager suitors, and her father invites them to write down the terms of their marriage offers in a letter, which he then, in a uniquely enlightened manner, sends to his daughter so that she can choose a husband herself. Apollonius conveniently acts as the letter's courier. She responds immediately by writing back to her father, who reads the letter aloud to the suitors, but since conventional feminine modesty keeps her from actually mentioning her beloved's name, they are confused by her indirect reference to "the man who lost his inheritance through shipwreck." The king turns to his daughter's tutor for help in interpreting the words, and the young man's blushing embarrassment betrays him. Fortunately, the king is happy to give his blessing to the marriage, and the love story ends, unsurprisingly, with a "happily ever after."

Prose fiction in the Second Sophistic offered fertile ground for the development of epistolary devices. Because of space constraints, the selections below are limited, chosen somewhat subjectively; the interested reader is encouraged to read further. Many other ancient novels include epistolary segments: Antonius Diogenes' *The Wonders Beyond Thule*; Heliodorus' *Ethiopian Story*; Iamblichus' *Babylonian Tale*; Xenophon's *Ephesian Tale*; and the complex narrative of the *Alexander Romance*, which possibly originated as a collection of letters (Stoneman 1991: 1–27). The authors of the Second Sophistic were fascinated by the power of writing itself, and we can see this clearly reflected in their experimentation with embedded epistolary forms as yet another way to vary narrative voice, introduce plot twists, and play with modes of communication between separated lovers. More than in any other genre, the letter seems comfortably at home in the novel, whether it is used for insight into a character's emotions or more kinetically (Altman 1982: 7–8; Jost 1966), as a means to instigate the action itself.

LETTERS AND PROSE FICTIONS OF THE SECOND SOPHISTIC: THE TEXTS

Lucian

"A True Story" 2.29, 35–6

At that point Odysseus, approaching me without Penelope noticing, gave me a letter for Calypso, to take to her on the island of Ogygia. Rhadamanthus sent the pilot Nauplius with us, so that if we landed on the islands, nobody would arrest us, assuming we were sailing there on some other business . . .

On the third day out we came near the island of Ogygia and landed. But before doing that, I opened the letter and read through the message, which was as follows:

> Odysseus to Calypso, greetings. I want you to know that after I built the raft and sailed away from you, I was promptly shipwrecked, and barely managed, with Leucothea's help, to survive and reach the land of the Phaeacians. They transported me back home, where I discovered my wife's many suitors carousing in my halls. I killed them all, but in turn was later killed by Telegonus, the son I had with Circe. And now I'm on the Isle of the Blessed, regretting very much

that I gave up the chance of spending my life with you and experiencing the immortality you offered. So if I can manage it, I'm going to run away and come to you.

This is what the letter said; it also asked her to entertain us as guests. So I walked a short distance from the sea and found the cave, which fit Homer's description perfectly, and there was Calypso hard at work spinning wool. After she took the letter and read it through, she cried for some time, but then she invited us in as guests, fed us magnificently, and asked lots of questions about Odysseus and Penelope—what she looked like and if she was really as virtuous as Odysseus used to claim she was in the old days. We answered her in ways that we thought might cheer her up. Afterwards we went back to the ship and slept next to it on the shore.

"Letters of Kronos" 31–9 (= "Saturnalia" 3–4)

Kronos sends greetings to the rich people. The poor people just wrote to me complaining that you don't share your wealth with them, and they asked me quite simply to distribute the good things equally to all people and let each person have his share. They said it was only fair to establish equal privileges, and not for one man to have more and another less of the good stuff. So I answered that Zeus would be the appropriate one to take care of that request, but my responsibility was to arbitrate their immediate concerns, in particular the injustices they thought they were suffering at my festival, and I promised to write to you on this subject.

Their requests strike me as reasonable. "How," they say, "can we possibly celebrate your festival if we're too busy shivering with cold and hunger?" They said that if I wanted them to participate in the festival equally, I should order you to hand over some clothing, perhaps some pieces you don't need or don't like, and you should sprinkle a little gold on the clothes for them. If you do that, they promise not to argue with you anymore in front of Zeus about your wealth; but if you don't do it, as soon as Zeus convenes court, they threaten to call for a redistribution of property. This charity shouldn't be hard for you to do, since you're so well off.

And by Zeus, I almost forgot, about those dinner parties where they dine with you—they also wanted me to include this issue in my letter. As it is, you dine extravagantly behind closed doors, and if every now and then you're willing to invite one of them in, the party brings more misery than good fun, and you try hard to find ways to insult them. It's pretty nasty, for example, when you don't let them drink the same quality wine as you do, by Heracles. I suppose you could fault them for not just getting up in the middle of it and going home, leaving the party entirely to you. But they say that they never even get enough to drink, and that the slaves who pour the wine have stuffed their ears with wax, like Odysseus' crew. And it just gets worse; I don't even want to mention their complaints about the division of food, and the servants who stand next to you until you're completely full but race past them, and all the other shabby things you do, totally inappropriate for respectable men. You know the best and friendliest attitude is one of equality, and the head waiter supervises your feasts just for this reason, so that all men can have an equal share.

So make sure that they don't have any more cause for complaint, but instead love and respect you as they share these few things. The expense will be minimal for you, but they won't ever forget your help in their time of need. And let me point out that you couldn't even live in your cities if you didn't have poor people as fellow citizens, contributing in countless ways to your happiness; nor would you have anyone to admire your wealth, if you grew rich alone, in privacy and secrecy. So let them all stare and marvel at the silver on your tables, and when you drink toasts of friendship, let them interrupt their drinking to examine the cup: guessing how much it weighs, checking the accuracy of the story depicted on it, estimating how much gold decorates the work. They'll stop envying you and start calling you kind and generous; after all, who could envy a man who shares his property and distributes things fairly, and who wouldn't pray for that man to live a very long life enjoying his good fortune? As things stand now, your happiness is unattested, your wealth envied, and your life unpleasant. I'm sure it can't be as satisfying to stuff yourselves with food in solitude, as I've heard lions and solitary wolves do, as it is to be in the company of clever men who try hard to please. First of all, they don't allow your party to be deaf and dumb; they'll be there with party jokes, harmless anecdotes, and all sorts of cheerfulness. This is the best way to spend your time, in harmony with Dionysius, Aphrodite, and the Graces. Then the next day they'll tell everybody about your generosity and increase your popularity. You'd spend a lot to buy this kind of service, but this way you get it free.

Let me ask you something. If poor people walked around with their eyes closed—let's just suppose they did—wouldn't you be upset that nobody was admiring your elegant clothes, your crowd of supporters, and the size of your rings? I won't even mention the plotting, the hatred you inevitably arouse in the poor against yourselves if you decide to enjoy your wealth alone. The curses they threaten to call down on you! I hope they're never forced to carry out that threat, because then you'll taste neither meat nor cake, except whatever's left over by the dog; your lentil stew will have salted fish floating around in it, your roasted pork and venison will plot an escape from the kitchen to the mountains, and your birds, even though they're wingless, will fly at full speed—fly away now!—to the homes of those very same poor people. But the worst of it will be that the most beautiful of your wine pourers will go bald in an instant, after having broken the wine jar.

So now think of some plans that are suitable for the festival and safest for yourselves. Lighten their heavy load of poverty, and at little cost to yourselves you'll have worthwhile friends.

The rich people send greetings to Kronos. Do you think you're the only one the poor people have written to, Kronos? Isn't Zeus already completely deaf from their shouting about these things? They think there should be a redistribution of wealth, they blame fate for making unfair divisions, and they accuse us of not wanting to share with them. But Zeus, being who he is, knows who's at fault, and therefore ignores most of what they say. Nevertheless, we'll offer you an explanation, since you're in charge of us now during your festival.

We've got your letter right here in front of our eyes: you wrote how it would be a good thing to help the needy with our riches, and that it would be better to mingle and celebrate with the poor. Well that's what we always used to do, treating everyone equally, so that not even our fellow feaster complained about a thing. At the start they said they only needed a little, but once we opened the doors for them, they never stopped asking for more and more. If they didn't get everything they asked for right away, they were angry, spiteful, and quick to curse us. And if they spread lies about us, people believed them, assuming they knew best because they'd been in our company. So we had two options: to stop sharing and let them utterly hate us, or to give all our property away and immediately become completely impoverished, one of the needy ourselves. At dinner, poor people didn't bother so much about filling up and satisfying their hunger, but when they'd had a bit too much to drink, they'd grab the hand of a pretty slave boy who was trying to give them back their wine cup, or they'd try to seduce your mistress or your wife. Then they'd vomit all over the dining room and come back the next day to insult us, claiming that they were dying of thirst and starvation. And if you think we're lying about this, remember Ixion, your very own dinner guest, whom you thought worthy of a place at the table, and who enjoyed equal honor with you—didn't that fine friend get drunk and assault Hera?

This is the kind of thing that has convinced us, for our own safety, not to let them enter our homes any more. But if they promise you to ask only for reasonable things, as they now claim to be doing, and not to act inappropriately during dinner parties, then let them join in and celebrate with us. Good luck to them. And just as you ordered, we'll send some clothes and spend in advance as much gold as we can, so that we won't be seen in any way deficient in our response. In return, let them stop being deceitful in their interactions with us, and let them be friends instead of flatterers and parasites. You won't find anything to blame us for if they're willing to do what's required.

Phlegon of Tralleis

"The Book of Marvels: A Ghost Story"

[During the reign of Philip, in the town of Amphipolis, a young woman named Philinnion, daughter of Charito and Demostratus, dies while still a young bride. Six months after her burial, she returns to life, and for several nights secretly meets with a young man named Machates, visiting from Pella as a guest of her parents.]

. . . she [the nurse] comes to the doorway of the guest room, and by the light of a lamp she sees the girl sitting next to Machates. The amazing scene seems to be playing tricks on her imagination; she can't wait any longer, but runs to find the girl's mother and shouts in a loud voice: "Charito! Demostratus!" She thought that the parents should get up and go with her to see their daughter, who was alive and sitting beside the guest in his room, by the grace of some god. When Charito first heard the incredible news, because of the serious implications of the message and the nurse's obvious distress, she was terrified and almost fainted; but she quickly regained control of herself and began to weep for her daughter; in the end she accused the old woman of being crazy, and ordered her to leave at once. But the nurse, speaking freely and reproaching her mistress, insisted that she herself was perfectly sane, even if her mistress was hesitant or even unwilling to see her own daughter. So Charito was just barely convinced, partly by the nurse and partly by her own curiosity about what had really happened, to go to the guest room.

Since some time had passed—two hours from the delivery of the original message—it was quite late at night when Charito arrived, and it turned out that the couple had already fallen asleep. As she peeked in, the mother thought she recognized her daughter's clothes and the outlines of her face, but since she couldn't be sure she was right, she decided to keep quiet. She was hoping to get up early the next morning and catch the girl, or, if she was too late for that, to question Machates about the whole thing, since she didn't think he would lie about something so important. So she silently crept back to her room.

At dawn, however, it turned out that the girl, either on her own or with divine help, had slipped away without anyone noticing. Charito entered the room, upset with the young man because her daughter had escaped, and after explaining the whole story from the beginning, she grabbed Machates' knees and begged him to tell the truth and hide nothing from her. The young man was worried and upset at first, but then grudgingly confessed that the girl's name was Philinnion. He reported how her visits began, and revealed that she was so in love with him that she admitted she came to his room without her parents' knowledge. In order to make his story more believable, he opened a small box and took out some objects the girl had left behind: a golden ring he had received from her, and the cloth belt she'd forgotten to take with her the previous night. When Charito saw these items, she screamed, tore her clothes, and ripped off the scarf that was covering her head; she collapsed on the ground, starting to mourn all over again as she clutched the tokens. The guest watched all this happen, noticing how everyone was deeply moved, weeping as if they were about to bury the girl all over again. He was affected himself, and begged them to stop, promising to show them the girl if she visited again. Charito was persuaded to calm down, but she warned him not to break his promise to her.

Night fell, and it was time for Philinnion's customary visit. Everyone in the household was watching, eager to learn of her arrival; and she came. She arrived at the usual time and sat down on the bed, but Machates pretended nothing was wrong, since he wanted to discover the truth of the whole unbelievable situation: could this person he was spending time with, who always arrived punctually at the same time, really be a corpse? After she ate some food and drank wine with him, he decided he couldn't believe what he'd heard from the others; he figured that some gravediggers had dug up the dead girl's tomb and sold her clothes and gold jewelry to this girl's father. But since he really wanted to find out exactly what was going on, he secretly sent slaves to get the parents, Demostratus and Charito. They arrived quickly, and as soon as they saw her they stood speechless, stunned by the unbelievable scene in front of their eyes; then they shrieked loudly and hugged their daughter. Philinnion said to them: "Mother and Father, you've been unfair in begrudging me the three days I just spent with this guest in my father's house; I wasn't harming anyone. So because of your meddling curiosity, you'll both experience the same grief all over again; now I'm going back to my appointed spot in the underworld, for I didn't come here against the will of the gods." As soon as she finished her speech she fell down dead, and they could see her corpse lying stretched out on the bed. Her mother and father flung themselves on the body, and the house was completely filled with loud cries and confusion because of the horrible experience.

It was an awful disaster, and the event itself was so hard to believe that the affair quickly became known throughout the city and was then reported to me. So all that night I held back the crowds that gathered around the house, worried that something bad might happen with such rumors being spread about. Even before daybreak, the theater [where they gathered] was full of people. After everything had been explained, it seemed best first for us to go to the tomb and open it to see whether the girl's body was in the grave or whether the place was empty. The girl hadn't even been dead six months yet. When we opened the vault where all the deceased family members were buried, on some of the platforms we saw bodies lying, and in other more ancient spots we saw bones, but on the platform where Philinnion had been placed for burial, we found only two things lying there: the guest's iron ring and a gold-plated wine cup, both of which she'd received from Machates on their first evening together. We were amazed and shocked; we immediately went to Demostratus' house to discover if it was true that the corpse was laid out for all to see in the guest room. Once we saw her body lying there on the ground, we rallied together in the assembly hall to figure out how to respond to such an unfortunate and unbelievable series of events.

There was total confusion in the assembly, and almost nobody was able to make sense of the matter. The first to speak was Hyllus, who we all know is not just our best seer, but also the most skilled in bird augury, and in general unusually talented in his profession. He stood up and declared that the girl should be buried outside the city limits, and that it wouldn't be proper to bury her again inside the city. We were also supposed to make a propitiatory sacrifice to Hermes the guide of souls, and to the Eumenides. Then he ordered us to purify ourselves thoroughly, to clean out the temples, and to do what was proper for the underworld gods. Then in private he recommended that I sacrifice to Hermes, to Zeus the god of strangers, and to Ares, all on behalf of the king and his affairs of state, and that I should consider all of it equally important. When he'd announced these things, we did as we'd been told. But Machates, the guest who was visited by the ghost, sank into a severe depression and took his own life.

If you think it's a good idea to write to the king about these events, write to me, too, so that I can send you one of the people who was closely involved in finding out the truth of the matter. Farewell.

Chariton

"Chaereas and Callirhoe" 4.4–5; 8.4–5

[Chaereas discovers that his former wife, whom he believed dead, has remarried; his current master Mithridates, governor of Caria, who is plotting on his own behalf, advises Chaereas to write a letter to her.]

[Mithridates said] "I think you just don't understand what Eros is like—he's a god who loves deception and trickery. So first you should try sending a letter to Callirhoe to find out if she remembers you and wants to leave Dionysius or 'wants to strengthen the house of the man who marries her' [Hom. *Od.* 15.21]. Write her a letter; let her be sad; let her be happy; let her search for you; let her summon you. I'll figure out how to deliver the letter. You just go away now and write."

Chaereas followed his advice, and when he was completely alone he wanted to write but couldn't; he was crying too much and his hands were trembling. After complaining about his bad luck, he struggled to start the letter as follows:

> To Callirhoe from Chaereas. I am alive, thanks to my benefactor Mithridates. I hope he'll be your savior too. I was sold into slavery in Caria by barbarians who burned that beautiful trireme, your father's flagship. Our city had used it for sending off a search party for you. I don't know what happened to the rest of the men, but my master's compassion saved me and my friend Polycharmus when we

were about to be killed. Mithridates has shown me every kindness, but he's also hurt me beyond reason by telling me about your marriage. I was expecting death, since I'm only human, but I never imagined you would get married. I'm begging you to change your mind. I'm pouring out tears and kisses on this letter. I'm Chaereas, your very own, the one you saw when you went as a virgin to Aphrodite's temple, the one you stayed awake nights for. Remember our marriage bed and that holy night when we first knew each other as husband and wife. But then I was jealous; well, that's to be expected in a lover. And I've paid the penalty: I was sold, enslaved, locked up. Don't hold a grudge because of that reckless kick of mine. I've been crucified on your account, and I didn't say a word against you. If you still remember me, all my suffering was worth it; but if you ignore me, then you'll deliver the death sentence.

Mithridates gave this letter to his loyal slave Hyginus whom he'd put in charge of his whole estate in Caria and who knew all about his love [for Callirhoe]. Mithridates himself also wrote to Callirhoe, revealing his sympathy and concern, claiming that he had saved Chareas for her sake . . .
[The letters are intercepted and delivered to Dionysius of Miletus, Callirhoe's rich and powerful new husband.]
Dionysius happened to be entertaining the most illustrious of his citizens. The feast was splendid: there were flutes playing and songs being sung. In the middle of this someone handed him a letter:

Greetings from Bias, general of Priene, to his benefactor Dionysius. Wicked slaves stole these gifts and letters en route for you from Mithridates, governer of Caria. I arrested them and have sent them on to you.

Dionysius read the letter in the middle of the party, noting with pleasure the mention of royal gifts. He ordered the seals to be broken and started to read the letters. Then he saw the words "To Callirhoe from Chaereas. I am alive." "His knees became weak, and his dear heart" [Hom. *Il*. 21.114], and darkness spread over his eyes. But even as he fainted, he kept a tight hold on the letters, fearing that someone else might read them.
[After many further adventures, Callirhoe inadvertently becomes the love interest of the King of Persia, Artaxerxes, who was supposed

to have arbitrated between Chaereas and Dionysius. At war in Egypt, Chaereas defeats Artaxerxes in battle and wins back Callirhoe. At the end of the novel, Chaereas writes to Artaxerxes, and Callirhoe sends a final secret letter to Dionysius.]

Chaereas also wrote this letter to the king:

> You were about to judge the case, but I've already won in the eyes of the best judge: war can best distinguish between the stronger and the weaker. War has returned to me not just my wife [Callirhoe] but yours too [Statira]. I haven't delayed as you did; instead, without your asking, I'm returning Statira right away. She's unharmed, and was treated as a queen even in captivity. You should know that Callirhoe is responsible for this gift, not I. We're asking a favor in return: give amnesty to the Egyptians. It suits a king to be charitable above all else. That way you'll have good soldiers who love you, since they chose to work for you rather than to follow me as friends.

That's what Chaereas wrote. But Callirhoe also thought she should write a thank-you letter to Dionysius. This was the only thing she did without Chaereas' knowledge, and knowing his jealous nature, she tried hard to keep it secret from him. Picking up a writing tablet, she penned the following:

> Callirhoe greets her benefactor Dionysius. I call you this [instead of husband] because you're the one who rescued me from pirates and slavery. Please don't be angry. I'm with you in spirit through the presence of the son we share; I leave him in your custody to raise and educate in a manner worthy of both of us. Don't expose him to a step-mother. You have not only a son, but also a daughter, and two children are enough for you. When he grows up, marry them to each other, and send him to Syracuse so that he can visit his grandfather. Give my regards to Plangon [a slave who had befriended her]. I've written this with my own hand. Farewell, good Dionysius, and remember your Callirhoe.

Sealing the letter, she hid it in the folds of her dress, and when it was time to sail and everyone was boarding the ship, she gave her hand to Statira and helped her on board . . . then as Callirhoe turned to leave, she leaned towards Statira and, blushing, gave her the letter, saying, "Take this letter to poor Dionysius . . ."

Achilles Tatius

"Leucippe and Clitophon" 5.18–21

In the middle of the feast Satyrus indicated that he wanted me to come over; his face was very serious. So I faked a stomachache and left the party. When I approached him he didn't say a word, but handed me a letter. I took it, but even before reading it I was totally shocked, because I recognized Leucippe's writing. This is what she wrote:

> To my master Clitophon, from Leucippe. That's how I have to address you, since you are my mistress' husband now. You know how much I've suffered on your account—or do I need to remind you? For your sake I left my mother and took up wandering; for your sake I was shipwrecked and captured by pirates; for your sake I became a sacrificial victim, an offering of atonement, and even died not once, but twice; for your sake I was sold and chained, lugged a shovel, dug up the earth, and was whipped. Did I do all this so you could marry another woman and I another man? No, it can't be. Through all these difficulties, I endured to the bitter end; but you, without being sold or whipped, have gone off and gotten married. If you are at all grateful for what I've suffered for your sake, make sure your wife sends me home as she promised. Let me borrow the two thousand gold coins that Sosthenes paid for me, and use it as bail until I can send the money back to [your new wife] Melitte. Byzantium is near enough. Even if you have to pay back the amount yourself, consider it payment for the suffering I've endured on your account. Farewell, enjoy your new marriage. I'm still a virgin as I write you these words.

Receiving this message, I became extremely emotional: I burned, I turned pale, I was amazed, I didn't believe it, I was delighted, I was upset. I said to Satyrus: "Did you bring this letter from Hades, or what does this mean? Has Leucippe come back to life? . . . Look, she reproaches me in her letter." I read through it again, line by line, imagining I could see her in it. "You're right to reproach me, dearest:

you've suffered everything because of me, and I'm the source of all your misfortune." When I read again the details of whipping and torture at Sosthenes' hands, I cried as if I could see the very acts in front of me. My imagination placed the eyes of my soul on the message in the letter, and it was as if I could see the things happening as I looked. I blushed deeply at her reproaches about my marriage, as if I had been caught, an adulterer in the act of adultery. Her letter made me feel deeply ashamed.

"Satyrus," I said, "how am I going to explain myself? . . . Tell me what I should write; I'm so upset by what's happened that I'm completely helpless." Satyrus answered: "I'm no smarter than you are, but I suspect the god of Love himself will dictate the words. Just hurry up now." So I started to write:

> Clitophon greets Leucippe. Greetings, my mistress, Leucippe. I'm sad and happy at the same time, because the letter shows you present even though I know you're still absent from me. If you can wait for the truth to be told instead of convicting me ahead of time, you'll find out that I've imitated your virginity, if there is such a thing as virginity for men. But if you already hate me, without hearing my explanation, I swear by the gods who saved you that soon I'll explain the whole affair. Farewell, my dearest, and be kind.

I handed the letter to Satyrus, begged him to say nice things to her about me, and then returned to the feast.

"The Story of Apollonius King of Tyre" 19–21

A few days later the king led Apollonius by the hand to the forum, where they walked around together. Three young students from very good families, who for a long time had been asking to marry the king's daughter, all greeted him in unison. When the king saw them, he smiled and said, "Why did you all greet me in unison?" One of them answered: "We've been asking to marry your daughter, but you've worn us out by delaying your decision so often. So we all decided to come together today. Choose which one of us you want as a son-in-law." The king said "You've caught me at a bad moment; my daughter only has time for her studies, and because her love of studying has exhausted her, she lies sick in bed. But so you don't think I'm delaying things even longer, I want you each to write your name and the terms of your offer in this letter; I'll send my daughter the letter, and she can choose a husband for herself." So the three young men wrote their names and the terms of their offers. The king took the letter, sealed it with his ring, and gave it to Apollonius, saying, "Take this letter, since you're her teacher, and give it to your student, if you don't mind. I could use your help here."

Apollonius took it, proceeded to the king's palace, went into the girl's bedroom, and handed over the letter. The girl recognized her father's seal, and said to her beloved, "My teacher, why have you entered my bedroom alone like this?" Apollonius answered her, "Mistress, you aren't even a woman yet, and you still take offense! Why don't you take this letter from your father instead, and read the names of your three suitors?" So the girl unsealed the letter and read it, but after reading it through, she didn't find the particular name she expected, that of the man she loved. She looked up at Apollonius and said, "Apollonius, you're my teacher; doesn't it bother you that I'm going to be married?" Apollonius said, "Not at all; I'm grateful that you've learned a lot from the studies I've helped you with, and now, by the grace of god, you'll marry someone your heart desires." And the girl answered him, "My teacher, if you loved me, you would certainly regret your teaching." Then she answered the letter, sealed it with her ring, and gave it to the young man. Apollonius took it to the forum and handed it over to the king. The king took the letter, unsealed it, and opened it; his daughter had written back as follows:

> Good king and best of fathers, since you are kind and indulgent enough to let me speak, I will reply. I want to marry the man who lost his inheritance through shipwreck. And if you're wondering, father, how such a modest girl could write so immodestly, let me add that I sent my message in wax, which has no sense of shame.

After reading through the letter, the king didn't know which shipwrecked man she was talking about. He looked at the three young men who had written their names and the terms of their offers on the letter, and asked them, "Which one of you was shipwrecked?" One of them by the name of Ardalio said, "I was." But his friend answered, "Shut up, and may the plague destroy you! I know you're exactly my age, you went to school with me, and you've never set foot outside the city gates. So where were you shipwrecked, then?"

And when the king couldn't figure out which one of them had been shipwrecked, he looked at Apollonius and said, "Apollonius, take this letter and read it, sir. Since you were there when she wrote it, maybe you'll be able to understand what I can't." Apollonius took the letter and read it; when he realized that the princess loved him, he blushed. The king took his hand, drew him slightly away from the other young men, and said, "What is it, Apollonius? Did you figure out who the shipwrecked man is?" Apollonius answered, "Good king, if you permit me to speak, I have." As he spoke, the king saw his face blush bright red, and he understood what he meant . . .

4

THE EPISTOLARY
NOVELLA

INTRODUCTION

The two epistolary collections translated in their entirety below are really a subset of the pseudo-historical letters that will be presented in the following chapter. They are attributed to famous figures from the past, and while the fifth-century Athenian politician Themistocles is better known to most modern readers than the fourth-century tyrannicide Chion, both would have been familiar names to ancient audiences. The *Letters of Themistocles* and *Chion of Heraclea* consist of freestanding epistles with no connective narrative, and in both cases all the letters are from one sender to multiple addressees. As with all the pseudonymous material, historical accuracy is not the author's main concern; instead, these two collections explore the psychological developments of protagonists who unwillingly leave their homelands and face unexpected challenges in foreign lands. Their dramas unfold in letters home, as they express their political and philosophical viewpoints, complain about rude acquaintances or hostile hosts, request loans of cash, or just send their regards to family members. The Roman poet Ovid followed much the same impulse when he wrote the *Epistulae ex Ponto* (*Letters from Pontus*) and *Tristia* (*Laments*), two collections of verse letters composed while banished from Rome and addressed to his friends and family back home. Although Ovid writes in his own voice, he evokes a character very much like that of the exiled Themistocles.

But the two collections presented in this chapter differ from other pseudonymous letters (and the epistolary poems of Ovid) in one very important way: they reveal a level of artistic unity and design that tempts us to identify them as novels or autobiography. In particular, both collections focus on a specific period in the protagonist's life in which he is challenged by circumstances and develops psychologically in response to his situation. So instead of allowing rather random epistolary chatter, the *Letters of Themistocles* and *Chion of Heraclea* are structured in such a way that the closest generic affiliation appears to be the novel. In general terms, the expectation of a novel is that it should include coherent structure, systematic plot development, and consistent characterization of the hero. Both collections presented here seem to fit that description, with certain adjustments in the case of the Themistocles letters. But because the term "novel" carries with it so much other cultural and literary baggage, I offer here the less controversial term "novella." What follows is a brief introduction to our two ancient epistolary novellas.

The *Letters of Themistocles* are a collection of twenty-one letters written in the voice of the fifth-century Athenian politician **Themistocles**. Purportedly composed during the period of Themistocles' ostracism from Athens on charges of political treason (ca. 472 BCE), they chronicle his fluctuating relationships with friends and acquaintances as he travels from Greece to Persia. Whoever composed these letters may have been partly inspired by Thucydides' quotations of Themistocles' letter to the Persian king Artaxerxes (Thuc. 1.137) and Pausanias' correspondence with that king's father, Xerxes (Thuc. 1.128–30), but the whole collection obviously also owes a great deal to Roman rhetorical exercises (Podlecki 1975: 129–30). Little is known for certain about the origin or authorship of these letters: there may have been one author or several, and the Greek text is badly preserved and at times clumsily written: one critic speaks of "tortuous and elliptical forms of expression, an excessive love of antithesis, and a predilection for metaphor and paradox" (Penwill 1978: 100 note 35). But most scholars agree on a probable date of ca. 100 CE. Although the collection cannot be proven to include any genuine correspondence of Themistocles himself, it is clear from other sources that Themistocles did write letters, especially during his periods of exile from Athens. So the idea of an epistolary fiction built around his life and career, as with the case of Chion, would seem entirely reasonable to the reader.

One of the more intriguing hypotheses about both novelistic collections presented here is that their authors used other evidence, now lost, that might have given them deeper insight into the lives of their characters. In the case of the Themistocles letters, the fifth-century historiographers Charon of Lampsacus and Hellanicus of Lesbos, both approximate contemporaries of Herodotus, may have provided the epistolary author with factual information as a foundation on which to base his imaginative inventions (Lenardon 1978: 154–5). But scholars have been justifiably wary of quarrying the letters for new material about the historical Themistocles. Instead, they tend to focus on the literary purpose and function of the work. Should we read the *Letters of Themistocles* as a historical novel or short story in epistolary form, as a loose and superficially arranged collection of letters circulating in the name of Themistocles, or as an essay in letters on the subject of exile, possibly meant to appeal to Stoic circles? These models all point to the overarching question of organization and unity as a key to generic categorization.

There are two major organizational problems that complicate our impulse to categorize the Themistocles letters as novelistic. First, the letters do not seem to be arranged in a clear chronological sequence; and second, there are major inconsistencies between individual letters in terms of factual information and character portrayal. One way to answer both objections is not to map the sequence across the entire collection, but rather to divide it into two distinct segments. *Letters 1–12* are arranged in chronological order, as are *Letters 13–21*: each segment begins in Argos just after Themistocles has been ostracized, and concludes with Themistocles seeking asylum at the court of the Persian king (Penwill 1978: 85). Once we read the letters as two parallel units, it turns out that inconsistencies or contradictions appear between the units, but never within them. The two segments resemble one another, however, in that they share central themes, attitudes, and characters, both minor and major; these overlaps ensure that we don't read the two segments as wholly distinct stories.

One modern reader has suggested that we should approach this epistolary collection as a diptych, in which the second part runs parallel to the first while discussing the same issues from a different perspective (Penwill 1978: 101–2). Thus the author offers his readers two versions of the same man: the unscrupulous politician who lusts after power (*Letters 1–12*), and the noble statesman who dedicates his life to promoting democracy in Athens (*Letters 13–21*). *Letter 13* functions as a kind of linking device for the two parts: it begins with Themistocles expressing his anger at the ingratitude of the Athenians who have ostracized him, but it shifts halfway through to an acknowledgment that, although exile is making him wholly wretched and encouraging him to sympathize with the Persian side, he will, in his heart, always be faithful to the Greek cause. If we follow this line of argument, we then conclude that the *Letters of*

Themistocles can indeed be termed an epistolary novella; by means of the unique diptych structure, the author offers two possible responses of Themistocles to his unjust exile, and through this, a study of "two possible responses of everyman to unexpected and undeserved misfortune" (Penwill 1978: 103).

Because of the complex nature of its doubled structure, the "plot" of the *Letters of Themistocles* is difficult to summarize, but a brief overview may help the reader distinguish some basic patterns. The letters are sent from different locations that reflect the route of Themistocles' flight. In the first sequence, Themistocles writes *Letters 1* and *2* from Argos, then letters *3–5* en route to Ephesus, where he writes *Letters 6–11*, and finally *Letter 12* from Susa, in the heart of the Persian empire. In the second sequence, Themistocles writes *Letters 13–16* from Argos, *Letters 17–19* in Corcyra while fleeing the pursuing Athenians, and *Letters 20–1* in Magnesia, where the Persian king has installed him as governor. More than one letter is obsessed with the rise and fall of Pausanias, the Spartan politician whose self-promoting, ruthless ambition is presented as a foil to Themistocles' own misunderstood attempts at good government: thus *Letter 2* warns Pausanias of the fickleness of fate, *Letter 14* explicitly accuses Pausanias of betraying his country, and *Letter 16* tries to clear its author of any guilty association with Pausanias, emphasizing the difference in their characters. Other letters give the reader a glimpse of Themistocles' personal life: he confides in his friend Habronichus that he is afraid for his wife and children left behind in Athens (*Letter 4*), and writes twice to his banker Philostephanus about arranging a transfer of funds to reach him in Ephesus (*Letters 6* and *7*). The lengthy *Letter 8*, addressed to his close friend Leager, deals with the legal prosecution of Themistocles in Athens; Themistocles is so perturbed by the dishonesty and hypocrisy of his fellow citizens that he discloses here, for the first time, his decision to travel to Persia, effectively confirming the suspicions of the hostile Athenians that he is a traitor to their cause. *Letter 10* also alludes to his travels with a clever reference to the simultaneous act of writing: as he pens his message, Themistocles tells us, he is at that very moment sitting in a carriage on the way to Susa. By the time the first section comes to a close with *Letter 12*, Themistocles has been well received by the Persian king, and the Athenians have manipulated the evidence of his desperate attempt to find sanctuary in Persia in order to discredit him in the eyes of his former supporters.

While *Letter 12* ends with a sense of irritation and bravado ("I'm no longer a pitiable exile . . . so the rest of you can go hang yourselves"), *Letter 13* jumps back to the early days of his exile in Argos, portraying Themistocles as a loyal Athenian citizen driven to despair by unfortunate circumstances. In *Letter 15* he finds the courage to ask a friend what the Athenians really think of him, and whether he will ever be allowed back home; he tries to find consolation in Athens' prosperity, even if his own situation appears desperate. *Letter 16* continues the theme of Pausanias' guilt that we encountered earlier in *Letters 2* and *14*, but it includes an additional detail relating specifically to its epistolary context, namely Pausanias' ruthless method of keeping his correspondence secret. As we already learned from Thucydides, Pausanias' successful scheming was promoted by an elaborate personal postal system arranged with Artabazus: each time Pausanias sent a letter to the Persian governor, the messenger bearing the letter was murdered upon delivery, thus assuring the continued secrecy of both the information transmitted and the system itself. Pausanias is finally unmasked as a traitor when a worried messenger, on his way to Persia, breaks the letter's seal and reads his death warrant. *Letters 18* and *19* highlight the volatility of political alliances in Athens: Themistocles thanks a former enemy who is now working on his behalf to recall him, and accuses two former friends of failing to help him now that he is in exile.

Letter 20, one of the longest in the collection, would have made, to our contemporary sensibilities, a logical conclusion to the entire work: it describes Themistocles' experiences after he leaves Argos, chronicling his travels to Corcyra, Naxos, and the Ionian coast, and ending eventually in the Persian court. The Persian king promptly installs him as governor in Magnesia, but Themistocles reassures his reader that he will not abuse his power, and that he will never sympathize with his foreign host to the extent that he would lead an army against Athens itself: "Am I supposed to fight against Athens and to do battle with the man in charge of the Athenian fleet? Many other things will come about, but this? Never!" Themistocles' emotional outburst may suggest to the reader that he will choose suicide over dishonor, but the author does not leave us to ponder this idea long, as the collection ends instead with a short letter from Themistocles to a friend in Argos, requesting various mundane supplies. This last letter (*Letter 21*), surprisingly, is the only one in the collection that uses epistolary convention: it closes with the formula "farewell," as if to mark not just the end of an individual letter but also the entire collection itself. Interestingly, *Chion of Heraclea* will conclude with the same pattern of a lengthy emotional letter (*Letter 16*) followed by a shorter letter (*Letter 17*) that finishes with an explicit closing formula: "farewell." There may have been some aesthetic principle at stake that we can no longer appreciate.

Looking back over this summary, the unity and internal cohesion of each half come into clearer focus. Juxtaposing the two halves, it becomes clear that the work is just as carefully crafted into a unified whole. Thus, there is no duplication of factual material, and gaps in knowledge that appear in one segment are filled in by the other (Penwill 1978: 100). We are introduced to one man's two distinct personae, but what is unusual here is that we are not asked to reconcile them. The protagonist's varied and often conflicting reactions reveal his psychological development in the face of difficult circumstances, and range from paranoia, alienation, bitterness, and isolation to reassertion of faith, confidence, and loyalty to Athens. The developments are realistically portrayed and properly motivated. The kind of psychological complexity presented in the collection is actually quite modern: the reader may be made uncomfortable by the lack of clarity in the temporal and logical lines of narration, but this technique calls for sophistication on the part of the reader, and sensitively reflects the unhappy Themistocles' own inner turmoil and confusion at his unjust fate (Holzberg 1994: 36–7). The epistolary form is very well suited for this narrative style in that each new letter can introduce a new temporal or psychological angle without being overly concerned with transitions.

Many of the general comments made about the *Letters of Themistocles* can also be applied to the other epistolary novella presented in this chapter, namely *Chion of Heraclea*. The seventeen letters written in the voice of **Chion** reflect historical events unfolding in the mid-fourth century BCE. The letters purport to be from an aristocratic young man studying at Plato's academy in Athens, who writes to family and friends back home in Pontic Heraclea (northern Asia Minor). Individual letters offer glimpses into the daily life of Chion's apprenticeship as a philosopher. Over the period of a decade, the collected letters, organized chronologically and addressed mostly to his father, describe how he learns the value of a contemplative life and the importance of political freedom. More than just a schoolboy's notes home, however, the letter collection, because it is organized chronologically, reads as a kind of *Bildungsroman* with political as well as personal ramifications. When the correspondence breaks off, the protagonist puts down his pen to take up a dagger:

Chion, it is implied, returns to Heraclea to take part in a successful, but for him fatal, rebellion against the tyrant Clearchus.

Thanks to other, non-fictional ancient sources, we know that Heraclea was, in fact, taken over in 364/3 BCE by a tyrant named Clearchus, who was killed a dozen years later by a group of conspirators led by Chion (Malosse 2004; Düring 1951: 9–13). But the author of this letter collection cannot be the same man: the language and style combine classical Attic with late Hellenistic or early imperial forms, and other chronological inconsistencies rule out the possibility of authorship contemporary with the events. Scholars assume that this collection was written by an anonymous author with advanced rhetorical training, composing in the first or second century CE for a receptive audience of Greek speakers (Konstan and Mitsis 1990: 258, but cf. Malosse 2004: 100–4).

There are many ways for a modern reader to approach this epistolary collection. It could be read, as was the case with the *Letters of Themistocles*, as a variation on a rhetorical school exercise (*ethopoieia*). In this case, its novelty lies in its sequence—seventeen variations on similar themes—as well as in its epistolary form. It could be read as a kind of historical novel, brimming with scenes of travel and adventure, although lacking a romantic subplot; what a different work it would have been, too, if Chion had also fallen in love! In its enthusiasm for the topics of philosophy and civic virtue, the collection resembles the fourth "Platonic" letter, an epistolary treatise that argues for the practical role of philosophy (Konstan and Mitsis 1990: 275). Finally, with its implicitly heroic ending, the work may have been a kind of political manifesto to encourage others to rebel against cruel tyrants. Perhaps the best way to begin to read *Chion*, however, is to consider the impact of organization and plot on its overall narrative shape. Unlike the similarly pseudonymous collection of Phalaris, for example, which appears to be edited to resemble an arbitrary jumble of personal letters, Chion's letters create an internally consistent and tightly structured tale.

Chion's first letter announces his departure for Athens via Byzantium; the bulk of his correspondence covers details of his life in Athens; and his last letter (*Letter 17*) admits that his duty is to return home and fight tyranny. Six letters from Byzantium (*Letters 1–3, 14–16*) build a framework for his departure and return. The work is full of unifying literary devices: repeated imagery (*Letters 2, 3, 4, 12,* and *13* report bad weather; *Letters 2, 7,* and *8* are recommendations), foreshadowing (the violence in *Letters 4* and *13* anticipates Chion's death), pairings (*Letters 4* and *5* are on famous men), and the sustained focus on Chion's father as the main addressee. Philosophical themes, such as friendship, civic duty, and the value of a philosophical education, connect individual letters, as we watch Chion mature over a decade.

The collection shows itself aware of the special demands of epistolarity on prose narration. Just as the modern epistolary novel draws attention to the difficulties of sustaining communication, so the author of *Chion*, in the name of verisimilitude, frequently alludes to practical details of writing and sending. The slave Lysis delivers *Letter 1*, later returning to Heraclea with *Letters 7* and *12*; when slaves are unavailable, Chion uses merchants en route to Heraclea. Chion dashes off *Letter 4* when he discovers a ship about to sail towards Pontus, implying that on other occasions, much is left untold for lack of a ship or messenger, creating discontinuity in the epistolary chronology. But continuity is then re-established whenever the writer becomes himself a reader by alluding to letters he has previously received. Chion answers his father's questions (*Letter 11*), recalls their conversations (*Letter 3*: "you must remember when"; *Letter 15*: "I will follow your advice") and quotes earlier letters (*Letter 5*: "you wrote to me that"). Allusions to other voices or texts are an important dimension of the genre, as the epistolary experience, although predicated on an absent addressee, is inherently reciprocal. Our collection, of course, offers us only Chion's side of the correspondence, so such references are even more critical to our understanding of the story.

Other than the *Letters of Themistocles*, whose peculiarities are discussed above, this is our only extant example from Greek antiquity of a historically inspired prose fiction composed solely of letters, arranged for the most part chronologically, and containing a number of unifying themes and concepts; in other words, an epistolary novella. Chion as "hero" guides the plot, developing from a callow youth into a responsible citizen, interacting along the way with enemies, accomplices, and friends. Niklas Holzberg argues forcefully that *Chion of Heraclea* exhibits all the significant characteristics of an epistolary novel: gradual revelation of events, chains of motifs, an explanatory letter at the end of the collection (*Letter 16*), and a sense of humor and self-irony (Holzberg 1994: 32). But whatever our final decision is on their generic affiliation, both *Chion of Heraclea* and the *Letters of Themistocles* are included in this anthology first and foremost for their creative use of epistolary form.

THE EPISTOLARY NOVELLA:
THE TEXTS

"The Letters of Themistocles"

1. To Aeschylus

After leaving Athens and arriving in Delphi, I decided that, if the Athenians allowed it, I would settle down to live there. On the way, I bumped into some friends of mine from Argos: Nicias and Meleager, as well as Eucrates, who had recently spent time in Athens. They stood around asking me questions, and when they learned about my ostracism, they immediately grew angry and blamed the Athenians in particular. When they realized I was planning to settle in Delphi, they stopped accusing the Athenians and began reproaching me, saying they would be insulted if I didn't accept them as suitable people to share my bad luck. They also pointed out that my father Neocles had lived for a long time in Argos, and that I shouldn't dishonor the memory of his love for Argos and his Argive friends. They almost went so far as to praise the Athenians for making me pay an appropriate penalty. Finally they urged me to honor them with more than just an accidental encounter, and not to insult the good luck of our meeting up. Then again they pointed to the example of Neocles, saying how appropriate it would be for me to live in the same city and home as my father once had. So, Aeschylus, they convinced me and took me to Argos. Now that I've stopped fleeing and landed in Argos, I'm suffering greatly because I won't agree to rule the Argives. They want to force me to rule, and claim that I'm acting unjustly towards them if I don't assume power. But I'm perfectly happy not being considered to be a great man, and not just because I've already been hurt by that reputation, but also because it's enough for me to have benefited from those things when I had to.

2. To Pausanias

I have been ostracized, Pausanias, by the Athenians, and now I'm in Argos, so the Athenians won't suffer anything evil on my account. They thought that they would suffer, so I didn't delay any further (since it wasn't possible to wait any longer) but left Athens and relieved them of their fear. The Argives have embraced me as more than just another refugee, and they want to take advantage of the situation the Athenians formerly enjoyed. So they think I'm worthy of taking on the responsibility of the general command of all Argos. But they do me great injustice by refusing to let me be a refugee as the Athenians intended. I find it awkward to reject their enthusiasm for me, but it would be even worse to accept what they offer; if I were to pursue that course, people would think I'd been ostracized with good reason. It would be pretty close to an admission of guilt if I, who had been expelled by the Athenians for trying to take control, should flee Argos because I'm being forced to take control. But I think it would be totally futile, Pausanias, to head out and find another city to live in, if they try hard to push their appeal too strongly, because no matter where I go, I would have to be careful that things didn't end up as they did in Athens.

I don't know whether I should now be particularly worried and afraid for you, since you are doing so well. I've heard that you control almost the entire Hellespont as far as the Bosporus, that you're planning an attempt on Ionia, and that the king has already become very familiar with your name. We who pray for your continued good fortune would very much prefer that you hadn't accomplished quite so much. Don't push your good luck, Pausanias; don't ignore the fact that success often breeds bad luck for men. This has always been the case for all men, but especially for those who are ruled by the laws and the people. We take command as slaves of the masses, but once we are in a position of power, we are envied by those who granted us power in the first place. Then they destroy us, not sending us back to the same place we were before our rule, but, proving their authority and profiting from the instability of fortune, they dismiss their rulers, sending us off to exile or death. So those who want to prosper in the city should avoid this very thing most of all. You should consider, Pausanias, how you can be least affected by the huge change that will come about from your present good fortune. As for me, since I've experienced it all, I refuse to chase after good fortune anymore.

3. To Polygnotus

I'm running away as fast as possible, just as you suggested, Polygnotus; I've left Argos behind, and am currently at sea with my course set for Corcyra; our ships are fast but we're being held back [by the weather]. I'm sure you'll praise the messenger's speed, since he was sent out just when the Athenians dismissed the meeting of the assembly, which was not far into evening, as they say, and he had already arrived in Argos the very next day before noon. But I'm afraid that if the storm keeps up, it will ruin our advantage, and I may end up slower in my escape than the messengers in their delivery of the news. But if the Spartans find out about my escape, they'll decide to pursue me, and then Pausanias will suddenly be found innocent of the same charges that they will bring against me. Now you are my savior, Polygnotus, and neither storm nor Spartans will keep me from acknowledging my debt. I'm deeply grateful that you told me with all speed what the Spartans had done and about Aristeides' quick action, which he alone undertook on my behalf even though he's my enemy; I'm also grateful that you warned me that if I didn't escape, I would face the horrible fate of a death sentence, which has now indeed already been voted into effect. God is responsible for how this will play out, and he will decide whether I'll be able to pay you back, Polygnotus, in exchange for all your help.

4. Themistocles greets Habronichus

It doesn't seem strange to me, Habronichus, to suffer an unjust and unworthy fate in Athens (since it would be stranger not to suffer anything at all); but it is strange that, up to this point, the anger expressed by my city was short in duration and promptly regretted— or perhaps I should say your city, since my words refer to it already as belonging to someone else. But as for now—and you can see how intense the feelings of my fellow citizens are against me—they have voted against me even in my ostracism, accomplishing the unusual task of banishing someone already in exile. I know you're going to say, by Zeus, they don't even allow me to be an exile. And even I have figured out that my exile seemed to them too small a punishment to pay for a man who had accomplished so many important things for the benefit of their enemies; they thought it better to sentence me to death. For that reason they've sent bounty hunters from Athens to Argos to track me down, and the Spartans in turn are following them. It didn't bother me, Habronichus, when the Spartans followed the Athenians, but it does irritate me that the Athenians now follow the Spartans. The Spartan magistrates condemned Pausanias without even believing the Athenians' slanders. They refused to believe Pausanias' friends, or those with him who knew about the whole affair, and they barely believed the confession of Pausanias himself. But your Athenians trust all outsiders in their business affairs, even if they are enemies. I suspect that the reason for this is that it's sweeter for them to envy their friends than it is for others to hate their enemies.

But I'm not writing this in order to expose what the Athenians have gotten away with. If only, by the kindly gods, they could avoid being exposed! For now it's impossible for those who praise the Athenians to defend them, since what's called for here is a conviction by their detractors. Instead, it seemed appropriate for me to complain to you, my dear friend, and also to remind you that we need to pay attention to our own affairs, especially since we see the Spartans controlling the Athenians and voting in laws against their personal enemies in Athens. You know, my friend, the reason for their anger, which is directed equally against you and me, is that both of us acted as ambassadors and negotiated the plan of building a wall around the city. The man who accompanied us on the embassy, since he's an honest man and has properly appropriated as part of his war spoils the reputation of honesty in the minds of the Hellenes, has gained a reprieve from the Spartans because he has taken their side against me. So let him do what he wants; he's always been vengeful, hostile, and envious. As Callaeschrus once said about him, his manners resemble those of a fox even more than one could guess from the name of his hometown, which is *Alopeke* (Foxtown)! But you, Habronichus, should settle your present affairs, plan as well as you can for the future, and be careful that the Athenians don't think too well of you. Just act the way you always have, but make sure to hide any excessive wealth and be content not to be noticed.

That's enough advice, my good friend, for you about your situation. But as for my affairs here, obviously I'm worried about escaping the Spartan hunters with their dogs who've set off from home to catch me. I won't give in to the Athenians and end up defiling them with the curse of my blood guilt, or inflict some contamination on the city which can neither be cured nor conjured away by offering bronze statues, as the gods demanded from the Spartans in the case of Pausanias, but whose crime instead is potent and inescapable, worse than Cylon's. And I won't give in by allowing the Spartans a double delight,—no, make that a triple: first by getting revenge for the hatred caused by the embassy I led with you; second by claiming that our prevention of their injustice was a trick we pulled; and third, by purging away their pollution and sending a pure avenging fury onto the Athenians' heads through their unholy murder of me. The Spartans think that, because a Spartan king [Pausanias] betrayed them, they can minimize the shame they feel in front of the rest of the Hellenes if I, a general, appear to be punished in the same way by the Athenians on a charge of treason. But as I said, I'll make sure that none of this happens, at least to the best of my ability; you'll hear about all this, and I'll write to you about all the details—how I'll be on guard against evil plots by my fellow man, and all the rest—when everything turns out well in the end.

Now about what's going on in Athens, dearest friend of mine, I beg and entreat you to help me as much as you can, and to do so publicly: don't save the money for me or my children, but spend it wisely and carefully on my children and their mother; also, make sure that every day you try to figure out how to save the lives of Cleophantus, his sisters, and his mother for me. My daughter is your daughter-in-law, married to your son Lysicles, so she should be especially loved by you and cherished by him, if I'm considered worthy of this connection by marriage. If you don't think me worthy, just remember that in the past, this relationship was planned and hoped for, and you owe the rest of my family a certain amount of goodwill because of me. I don't think that the Athenians themselves would attempt an attack on my wife and children, even if I annoy them greatly and the resentment of those who hate me increases; nor would they enlist others to do their dirty work for them. But if there is even a slim chance or the slightest suspicion that they might, let me anticipate the worst and suggest right now an escape plan. You know Cleophantus' attendant, whose name is Sicinnus; he once helped me, too. He can arrange where they should be sent and how they should manage their escape. All he needs to know is that they can't stay in Athens; he'll understand the rest, and know what to do. I suppose I shouldn't hate the Athenians so much that I suspect they might do things they've never done before, nor, I trust, will ever do. But if it should come to that, I've shown you what you need to do (since it isn't excessive to remind you yet again of your duty in such a crisis), and I'm sure you'll do as I've commanded. So it seemed best for me to write you this letter as quickly as I could, and I'll write more about all this once I see what the future brings.

5. Themistocles greets Temenidas

At Admetus' house, things turned out a bit differently than you expected. When I got there, he wasn't home, but was off visiting the Chaones. I ran into your friends Cratesipolis and Stratolaus and gave them the letters. But Admetus returned fairly soon, no more than eight or maybe nine days later. I sat down at his hearth in suppli-cation (just as Cratesipolis had told me to do), holding his little son Arybbas in one hand and a sword in the other. Catching sight of the boy and me, Admetus recognized me immediately. I know well that he felt nothing but hatred, but he pitied the child and was terrified of the weapon in my hand. He raised me up but refused to let me stay in his house, claiming he wouldn't be able to keep me safe; he was afraid of the Athenians and even more afraid of the Spartans. But he promised to send me to a safe place, and he kept his word. I boarded one of Alexander of Macedon's merchant ships. The ship had reached Pydna at that point, and from there was scheduled to set sail for Asia. So that's the story of my arrival at and departure from Admetus' house. When you write from Argos, don't send the letter to Admetus himself (he didn't seem too eager to see me get away safely), but rather to Cratesipolis. She would enjoy a letter from you and also your sister, since I think she worries a lot about both of you, but you most of all.

6. Themistocles greets Philostephanus

I am sickened, Philostephanus, by your ingratitude and complete dishonesty toward me; and it bothers me even more that I was so stupid. People will say I was born and died an utter fool, because I was unable to assess and understand properly the habits of even this single man, as he sat at the crossroads of Hellas, with his morality laid bare, clearly recognizable through his actions. And yet I think it's because of me that you've become the wealthiest and most famous man not only in Corinth, but everywhere else where men use banks in their daily dealings. Before we were business partners, even if you weren't that rich, at least you were well trusted, certainly more trusted than you're likely to be considered now, since you've become rich with my help. So it's not my fault that I trusted a man whose character was so unexamined and unobserved; no, it was my own bad luck that he was never untrustworthy towards anyone who brought him a profit; but towards me alone, from whom he received so much money, he has acted unjustly.

You wonder where I got my facts? Tibius arrived just recently from Athens here in Ephesus and said that Meidon's men had sent him to me. He claimed they had to get seventy minas of silver from my accounts, that he was supposed to get this amount from you, and that it was just a tiny fraction of the entire sum of forty talents I owed. This, according to the last calculations we made together at the Isthmus, appeared to be the total final balance of my money that still remained with you. Tibius reported that when you read through my letter and realized that I needed money, you answered first kindly and appropriately, but then turned around and acted unkindly and shamefully—I could almost call it unholy. When you said that you wanted to send on as much money as I and my creditors needed as an outright gift, out of the goodness of your heart, rather than setting up a loan and becoming my money-lender, that was civilized and worthy of your fine feelings towards me. But when, as Tibius tells me, you became irritated and denied you owed me anything at all, you did something so bad that it outweighed all your previous kindnesses. Your generosity is worth seventy minas, but your wickedness adds up to a full forty talents.

But I can't abandon so quickly the idea that you really are a good and honest man (this could be the case even now, although I'm still reeling at how things turned out contrary to my expectations); if you were untrustworthy in a matter of trust and unjust when justice was called for not because you were shameless, or greedy for personal gain, but because you thought it would be advantageous for me if you denied my request, then you wouldn't be seen as an evil man, and you would concur that I wasn't a fool for letting you treat me this way. But if my suspicions are correct and you are dishonest, and all this is confirmed by the Athenians, you won't deceive the gods, Philostephanus, with your wickedness, nor will you get away with cheating me; and even if you have no respect for me and couldn't care less about the gods, in the end, you won't escape the Athenians. For in this whole affair, as in all other circumstances, I would prefer to be robbed of that much money by my own country rather than by Philostephanus, the money-lender from Corinth. So then write me a letter stating the nature of your relationship with me and how you've decided to proceed in the rest of this matter; then, if you really are my well-meaning friend, and you continue to be the man you used to be, I can make plans about saving my money to lessen my misfortune; and if you are not a friend, then explain how my money won't be lost against my better judgment.

7. *Themistocles to Philostephanus*

Menyllus, the ship's captain from Chalchis, the man who once brought into Piraeus' harbor that huge shipment of grain from Gelon of Syracuse, came to Ephesus, bringing me letters from you on the last day of Boedromion according to the Athenian calendar, and on the tenth of Panemus according to your reckoning (the two days are one and the same). He passed on messages in the form of riddles, and while he didn't understand the riddles, I did, because I recognized the code we had agreed on together. And he also delivered your letter. You seemed extremely upset and angry that I would ever think you could be untrustworthy or hostile towards anyone, much less towards me. Then you gave me a report on my financial affairs, not denying that you have the money, and promising that you would deliver it whenever and to whomever I should ask. You proved to me that Meidon and Pamphilus didn't fully understand the situation, and that Tibius was acting criminally. And I'm almost ashamed to admit, Philostephanus, since you've turned out to be so sensible, that I'm delighted not so much about the existence of the forty talents as I am about the fact that you haven't destroyed my faith in you. You should know that, even though you hadn't yet received the sum, you were about to return my forty talents; so I thought you were worthy of receiving not just that sum, but thirty more talents in addition. The largest amount of money I deposited with you then was seventy talents. Given that I entrusted you with the larger sum, I shouldn't necessarily be doubted if I seem to entrust you with a smaller amount. Now about my tendency to lose my temper quickly, I admit I shouldn't have been suspicious of such a good friend or so quick to accept the slander against you. When I say this, I am speaking the whole truth, Philostephanus; that criminal Tibius convinced me to turn against you, and fate made me believe him. That's enough about that topic. Keep the money at your house for the time being, and then when I've thought about the whole thing some more and come to a clearer decision, I'll write to you again.

8. Themistocles to Leager

It's quite something, Leager, how Leobotes of Argylae, and Lysander, son of Scambones, and Pronapes of Praseae now cheerfully embrace the people of Athens, who never before found them to be so loyal. They are so just and honorable that they went ahead and perjured themselves on a very serious issue: the betrayal of all Greeks. And now they pile immense credit upon themselves—something others wouldn't agree with—since they've not only avoided the suspicion and the condemnation that was directed at them and even declared formally, but they've also come out of this whole affair looking like honest and trustworthy men. Leager, my old friend and compatriot, son of Glaucon, you won't admire the Athenians for this (although you're free to admire and love them for other reasons), nor will you respect them, but you'll feel ashamed. All of you Athenians, Leager, won't go wrong in being grateful for your own salvation, which happened to be my misfortune. You offered me to the Athenians as an object to feast upon, since I had fallen like some great fat beast, hunted down. And in fact this, I dare say, was my only bit of good luck, since in all other respects I have fared so unspeakably badly. For by suffering what I suffered I did some considerable good to you, my friends. But to be cheerful, or even more, to rejoice in such a rescue, what right-minded man could endure that?

Didn't you yourselves proclaim the condemnation against me to all the Greeks, a charge as intolerable as it is disgusting, both unjust and completely untrue? It's true that Aristeides, Phaedrias, Tisinicus, and Alcmeonides perjured themselves, but didn't you also swear an oath? Oh gods and daemons who are witnesses of the truth among men, why didn't the statue of the goddess you swore by, and even the very temple itself fall down upon the heads of those criminals when they made you swear that oath? Do they trust you now because you swore your oath, even though they didn't trust you before? Then why didn't they make me take an oath, so they could trust me, too? And if they thought I was worthless but you were all good citizens, why did they charge you also, the good citizens, at the same time as me, the worthless one? For either a man's character or an oath sworn to a god should be trusted. Knowing your good character, they never should have put you under oath; and knowing your oath was to be trusted, they shouldn't have been stupid enough to question your character. None of this makes sense, Leager, and nothing is as they say it is. It's their envy of you that has caused the disturbances they talk of. They certainly don't need another Themistocles yet, since they're still preoccupied with me. And if, as is likely, the case against me succeeds, then I'm very much afraid for you, and you ought to be frightened on your own behalf that your oath might have no value; you thought they believed you, but you were wrong. How ridiculous it would be if I, whose oath is not believed, succeed in escaping the nets and the hunters, while you, acknowledged to be faithful and reliable, are so wronged and misrepresented by the witnesses.

Perhaps someone will say, "You frighten us, Themistocles, and scare us when you talk like that." Well, if I keep quiet, I don't frighten you, but if I do speak, you should listen to me, even if you didn't that other time—don't you remember, when I instructed all the Athenians to leave the city and persuaded them to embark on their ships? Even though they listened to me then, I didn't persuade those same people to allow me to live with them in Athens.

Why do I say "with them"? They wouldn't even let me settle outside Athens, somewhere else in Greece. I, the Pythian (that's what they called me when I interpreted the oracle for them), am not allowed a tiny piece of Delphi or Delos, and if it is up to them, not even of Xanthus, unless upon my death I might find a place at the edges of the world, among the Hyperboreans. Although the Greeks used to rise respectfully from their seats when I went to Olympia to view the athletic contest, now for this same man there is no possibility of honors or front seats at a festival or in the theater. There's no home for me in any community in Greece, nor am I allowed to be a suppliant or a refugee in a temple precinct. Aren't you scared by this, Leager, or struck by amazement? Or do you think that, since you took an oath, all will go well with you? If only it would, goddess Athena! But nothing is as unintelligible as when prayers and hopes make no difference in the outcome.

"What is to be done?" you will ask me. "Should we choose exile if nobody forces us to leave?" That's not what I'm saying. Instead, don't close your eyes for even a minute, don't trust anyone, and be on your guard. Circumstances will suggest to you when it's time to leave, if it's necessary, or whatever you need to do, as long as you're ready for action. But if you relax, thinking that you have matters under control, I'm afraid that I, in my misfortune, will lose all of Athens. Up to now I think I still possess something of Athens, and, by Zeus, not the worst part either, but the very best, as long as my friends survive and are still living there. But if I, a refugee, keep drifting wherever it may be on earth, and my enemies are famous and powerful, and you, my friends, couldn't remain there together, but had to leave behind small children orphaned and enslaved, destitute wives, both yours and mine, and old men and women, in some cases our surviving parents; if all this, I say, were to happen at once, wouldn't it be better for me to stay away and to suffer the fate my enemies want for me than to see any of this happen or to hear it talked about?

So, Leager, think about this day and night, and try to come to a decision; then encourage all our friends to do some planning and take action in this regard, not only those who have sworn an oath but also those who have not—you know all of them. You can show them everything in my letter up to this point, if you want, and read it to them. But either erase and destroy the section that follows, or cut if off and keep it, and let nobody know about it except you. For I realize that the game I'm playing here is bold, rash, and desperate, and maybe even extremely dangerous. Still, I've gambled that my daring plan will turn out well, and I stand by my decision. Neither will my friend Leager want to stop me from my efforts—he wouldn't be able to—nor will my father Neocles or my uncle Themistocles, if they came back to life and arrived at my side. No omen or augury will hold me back, not even if it came from the very man who prophesied to your fellow citizens that they should barricade themselves within a wooden wall. So wish me good luck, my friend, and pray to the gods to grant me deliverance, to give me a safe return journey, and to offer a conclusion to my enterprise that's not only what I hope for, but also what I deserve. For I've decided to sail from Ephesus straight to the Persian king, who is, as you know, our enemy but, at least according to the Athenians, my friend. By Zeus, let's hope they're clairvoyant and speak the truth! I have already been in touch with him by letter, and his answer to me by messenger was so courteous that I was completely amazed and greatly astonished, if only for the fact that I had never before communicated or written anything sincere to him. There would be no point in his imitating me since he is a powerful king, and it wouldn't be an advantage for him to harm me by lying, since he could do the same thing if he wanted to by telling the truth. So I'll go to him; what I am going to do if I can, I'm ashamed to say, but I wish to act if I can . . . [corrupt text] Please look after my affairs there as discreetly as possible, since that will help us both; be very careful, as I know well you will be. I'm more worried that you'll take care of my business openly than that you might handle it carelessly. Be careful in this, if you love me, not only for your sake, since you are as dear to me as my life, but also for my own sake, so that you may be useful and helpful to me for a long time to come. I've sent this letter to you expressing my views of the situation, and I'll try to indicate to you as soon as possible what happens next, so you'll know everything about what's going on with me.

9. Themistocles to Callias

Please, Callias, don't try to compete with Aristeides in jealousy; he said that he wasn't trying to compete with you in riches. But it's still far better, given what everyone prays will come about for themselves and their families, that you befriend Aristeides rather than imitate his actions, which everyone hates and considers evil. Now don't blame the Athenians or question their judgment, hinting to me that they vote randomly and select leaders from the worst pool of candidates. Take a moment to consider this: you're complaining because they've elected officials who have won, and whoever you are, making these silly accusations, you haven't been able to stand out of the crowd as a general like all those others including me. The city needed to choose chief commanders not from the group of men who robbed the graves of Persian corpses in the pits at Marathon, but rather from those men who fought at sea and killed the enemy drawn up in its ranks at Salamis and Euboea. The city didn't need men who had acquired huge riches but weren't willing to admit where or how they had acquired them; it needed men who had accomplished great and noble deeds. In the ways in which you were most able, more than anyone else, to help the city, you didn't help it one bit, yet in the ways you were least helpful of all the Athenians, precisely in those areas you tried to meddle and get involved. Since you had more money than countless Persians who had all passed on their inheritances to you, and since you stole the spoils from those who resisted them as well as from the entire city, I don't know how you got away with never serving your fatherland in any way, either big or small. But when it came to giving speeches, an area in which you are least talented, you try to scold Athens, and you blame the Athenians for deciding one way rather than another in their battle strategies, an area in which you are badly informed and quite cowardly. But this is the way it is, Callias. When the lion is still alive, neither bulls nor any other large courageous animal can stand firm against it, but when the lion is down and out, it's no surprise when even little flies crawl all over its body. So now you, too, enjoy doing whatever you want to me, gloating over the fact that I'm being trampled on by everyone. It will be no surprise, however, if at some later point, when I'm back on my feet and have regained my fighting spirit, god will grant that I remember your speeches against me. I'm sure he will grant it, since, as the poets say, bad deeds don't end well.

10. Themistocles to Habronichus

I've dared to do great and terrible things, Habronichus. Euxitheus came to you at my command, in order to tell you in person and reveal what I'd resolved to do. But you kept silent as he spoke, staring at the ground, unable to approve my plans, I suppose, but not wanting to impede them either. You did the right thing. You couldn't have prevented anything, and it wouldn't have been appropriate for you to curse me. But I'm off now, heading out, and I'm already sitting in my carriage as I write this to you. Farewell, and don't worry about me.

11. *Themistocles greets Ameinias*

Although we haven't known each other for long, it still seems as if we've been friends all our lives; the job we shared was so important that it was enough for us just to fight together on that day in the same battle at Salamis. And the two of us were more than just one tiny part of the army: I, whom you and the rest of the world alive today recognize easily, and you, the best ship's captain of the whole fleet. That's why our friendship is stronger and deeper than any that could develop between men who regularly eat meals together twice a day, even if they lived as long as they say old Tithonus did. When I think about how brave and honest you were, I'm convinced that you won't forget those things that you should really remember; I think you can still see in your mind's eye that critical moment when, thanks to my efforts, everyone congratulated you. But because I took your side, I offended many powerful men, not only Athenians, but other Greeks as well. How could it be any worse, given that, on the Athenian side, Alcibiades, Stratippus, Lacratides, and Hermocles, as well as Aristeides from Aegina, Dorcon from Epidaurus, Molon from Troezen, and many other Greeks judged me guilty of betraying my position of power as general? They exiled me from my own father-land [corrupt text] . . . They made the right decision when they honored your bravery, but at the same time they resented your success, and that's why I'm now being driven out of Athens and sent off into exile by the Athenians and many others [corrupt text] . . . Will your memory of past injuries, along with their injustice, wholly overcome the gratitude and just rewards that you owe me? Will those men who abuse me unjustly overpower those who justly treat me well? I don't believe you're capable of such things, Ameinias son of Euphorium; you're a man of noble blood, not only because of your father, but also because of your brothers: Cynegeirus, who stood out from all the rest in fighting at the battle of Marathon, and Aeschylus, who has been famous all his life for his learning and his goodness. But you'll be true to yourself; you'll follow in your brothers' foot-steps and rescue me, your leader, Themistocles. The best kind of help would be to stand your ground whenever the Assembly meets. And if anything new is being plotted against me in public gatherings, or, if the men who exiled me are planning to do something awful to my poor wife, you would be doing me a favor if you could promise to help me and to offer my family sufficient aid. If you promise to do this, you won't find it a burden; I'm asking only for evidence of your goodwill and sincere concern.

12. *Themistocles to Aristeides*

I've arrived in Persia, Aristeides, I've arrived, and they haven't mistreated me at all. I know that in your own mind you're amazed at this news, even though in public you pretend that my message reports nothing unexpected; you'll even use it to prove to the Athenians that the slander against me was justified, since I had such confidence in the Persians and they are now treating me as a friend. But when you spout forth such nonsense, I hope the victory statue set up at Salamis will fall down and crush you; it's stone, you know, large and plenty heavy. If some god, not just to punish your false pretensions, but also in the name of honesty and truth, were to hurl that stone statue on top of your accursed and ungrateful head, then, I suspect, you'd stop stirring up your fellow citizens and envying their other benefactors. The great king of Persia isn't sheltering me in return for my earlier kindness towards him (surely he would be the least likely person to do me any favors in exchange, considering what he suffered); no, he realized full well that I was his enemy in former times, but he was amazed at my courage and pitied my bad luck. So you're endangering yourself by coming on an embassy to the king about me. You treated me badly, but he would help an innocent victim; you made me an object of pity by exiling me, but he took pity, as it should be, on the exile. Actually, as things are now, I'm no longer a pitiable exile. So Aristeides, Lysimachus' son, can go hang himself, and the rest of you can go hang yourselves too, since you find no pleasure in the fact that I've met up with a happier fate than expected.

13. *Themistocles greets Polygnotus*

Of course, Polygnotus, when you think about my past leadership and experiences fighting at sea, you urge me to react to my removal from Athens just as courageously. As I set out, and when I saw before me what I was leaving behind, I promised myself that I would accept my exile bravely. When I thought about my experiences fighting at sea, and all the other similar challenges I'd survived, I was sure I would bear even this with great courage. And you know that I left without weeping too much. But now, Polygnotus, time brings with it neither forgetfulness of what I left behind nor any sense of growing used to my condition of exile. Certainly exile would be easy to bear if it weren't long term, but with time, the things I left behind become even more desirable, and I get no consolation from the fact that I've endured many other things bravely, fighting against the barbarians and risking my life. When I think about it, even these things have turned out contrary to my expectation. Really, I thought I took such risks so that I would be able to enjoy living in Athens; so all the more reason for me to get upset, Polygnotus, if many other people who weren't even present as spectators at the sea battles of Euboea and Salamis are now allowed to live in Athens and can banish and recall whomever they wish whenever it strikes their fancy, yet I, who helped the Athenians protect their authority even if only for a short time, am the only one who is deprived of both my authority and the right to live in Athens; instead I'm called an exile, a name which is sweetest to the ears of my worst enemies. I feel this more intensely because I've been abandoned by my friends and deprived of my home and hearth, where I once offered sacrifices in honor of my victory against the Persians. I'm a refugee in a strange land and city, and I'll probably die here, still stuck in exile. Indeed, would I have attacked the enemy so furiously if I could have predicted such an outcome? Would I have pursued this victory if I had realized it would bring with it such rewards? And after the Persians left, would I have risked offending the Spartans to protect the city of Athens? Now I must pray for blessings for the Argives [who've taken me in] and every other city out there, since every city except Athens would welcome me.

I'm compelled to say these awful things because of my exile: it's slowly driving me insane. What evil deed, Polygnotus, have the Athenians done to me, what that isn't good? Surely I must be lying, and my accusations about events will be dismissed. But if the Persians attack Attica again, I won't think I'm out of danger because I'm an exile, nor will I think that the challenge is just for those who haven't suffered so much already, but, even if I'm no longer a sea captain or a general of troops, Polygnotus, I'll fight as an exile. I won't be worse at riding or commanding a ship because of this; in fact, I might be even better at fighting because of my experiences. The worst of the Athenians might be able to force me into exile, but they could never force me to be a coward. Ironically, in the way the Athenians are punishing me I think I perceive the very authority I saved for them. So I think about these things often, and am full of a thousand ideas, and try to resist getting too upset; but my present state of exile lies heavily on my mind, dragging me into despair and overwhelming my emotions, and even leads me away from the previous strength of my convictions. Not even the many Argives here with me would deny that I'm suffering, and when compared to their large numbers, the absence of friends and family seems even more marked. But if your daughter has now recovered—since her illness was your excuse for delay—come and relieve me of my many griefs. And if something else holds you back, I pray that it will be resolved. Let's both persuade Megacles, you by being there with him and me by writing a letter, to stop just promising to come but rather to fulfill my hopes by actually coming here.

14. Themistocles to Pausanias

You have argued favorably in Fortune's defense, Pausanias; therefore, and because of your well-deserved misfortune, you've also deprived me of the opportunity to keep pressing my case against Fortune. Trying to become a Persian although you're really a Spartan, and plotting to annex Greece to the Persian empire, you've just deprived yourself of the authority you used to have in the Hellespont and the power you used to command for these tasks. But you're still going around hoping for a chance to accomplish what you had in mind. So you've mismanaged the Fortune you had before, rather than Fortune treating you badly. But even at this point, you're still in luck, because you're risking your life at just the right moment. Even if your fate is to be killed by the Spartans, you'll have the consolation that you won't have died without a good reason. You are closely allied with [the Persian governor] Artabazus, and you're eager to become the Persian king's son-in-law. Yet how can you think that there is an equal give and take here, when you receive a foreign wife and along with her some property—Carian land, or maybe Phrygian—, while you betray the whole land of Greece and its Greek cities, and you don't even exclude Sparta in the deal?

Do you really think, fool, you can get away with this? And if you don't succeed, do you think no one will notice because you only thought about betraying us, but didn't actually carry out your actions? But Pausanias, the coastlands of Troy and Colonae, where you've been hiding out and working together with the Persian king, are not so far away from the Peloponnese that your activities there go unnoticed. Gongylus, the worst of the Eretrians, has been acting as a go-between (if it's true you've been using him to carry messages back and forth). Such rumors are being brought back to Greece. You've also offended Mnastoridas, a man who is a Spartan and wants to remain a Spartan, and who has always lectured you about respecting the laws of Sparta. But you alone continue to enjoy being a traitor. But stop and think, you wretch, if Artabazus or the king's daughter who is now already ripe for marriage, will provide any benefit to those who call themselves Spartans. And let my letters to you be even harsher, since I, the person who reproaches you, am myself an exile.

15. *Themistocles to Autolycus*

I am less interested, Autolycus, in being consoled than in hearing the truth; but when you write that the Athenians already very much regret my exile, I think you're consoling me rather than telling me the truth. The men who've been slandering me to the people are as strong as ever, and there's been no opportunity to remove these evil men from power in the city, making sure at the same time that everyone understands that they've managed to throw out better men than those. But now they conceal and obscure their worthlessness as the city flourishes. I suppose I shouldn't complain about their machinations as long as the city prospers. Indeed, I should really be delighted at Athens' good fortune, even though it's just a rumor, and even if I wasn't responsible for it and won't benefit from it, since I've been in exile. Yet perhaps even this turn of events is the result of my time in office, and the good situation I established back then continues to function well today; and perhaps I should justly hold myself responsible for opening up such a wide and easy path for civic affairs that the city no longer needs a leader. But Autolycus, please don't write to me how you yourself hope the Athenians regret my exile, but rather how they themselves really feel. For I think the wicked men who are always present keep making them change their minds about me, and their wickedness would be even more obvious if I hadn't been exiled.

16. *Themistocles to Alcetas*

You used to think Pausanias' fate was a blessing, Alcetas, but that my exile was reason for grief; you often wrote that Fortune had abandoned me and attached herself to Pausanias. But that man has disappeared along with his good fortune. His great rule over the Hellespont has disappeared, his wealth and reputation that rivaled the king's have disappeared, and he didn't even have a proper burial when he died. The men who were most impressed by Pausanias are now the ones who are least likely even to mention his name, as if doing so would pollute those who were listening with an evil stain. So it's not appropriate any more for you to praise Pausanias' greatness or lament his current fall from favor. For he certainly got what he deserved, and I applaud his punishment. And if you're quite surprised when you realize how his fortunes were reversed, I'll tell you the real story so you won't be surprised any more [corrupt text] . . . You'll change your mind and be amazed that such a man survived, experienced good fortune at one time, and for a long period even enjoyed life.

Pausanias wanted to betray Greece to the Persian king; he loved all things Persian, imitated their lifestyle, and used to get frustrated that he was Greek instead of one of Persia's allies. When he seemed to have proved by his actions at Plataea that he wasn't a traitor, he was entrusted with the command of the Hellespont. And once he had that command, right away he defended himself to the Persians, claiming that he had acted bravely against his will at Plataea. He gave Greece over to them as payment for those actions, and he allied himself with Artabazus, who was the king's governor [satrap] among the tribes living on the coast, and he announced all this to the king himself. He was now himself a Persian, both in attitude and lifestyle; not even his clothes identified him as a Greek anymore. At first, as you surely know, few messages about this reached Sparta, but even though the information was limited, they were immediately worried, although not too seriously. But when he was recalled, Pausanias had to pay a fine, was relieved of his command, and went back to being a private citizen. He went immediately back to Asia, full of anger and resentment at being removed from his position as general, and began plotting even more energetically. But he still worked in secret, not out of embarrassment at potentially being discovered as a traitor, but out of the fear that he would fail if his plans were out in the open. Only once he had fully prepared his whole treasonous plot did he intend to go immediately and publicly over to the Persian king's side.

In the meantime, he invented a technique for sending secrets to the king, and it was by this very technique in particular that for a while he flourished, but then later was destroyed. Every time Pausanias sent a messenger to Artabazus, the man was killed after delivering the message. For Pausanias, not leaving any details of his treason up to chance, ordered every messenger to be killed so that there would be no evidence left about what he was up to. The technique worked well for him while he murdered three or four messengers, but when he tried it a fifth time, the attempt failed and was exposed. Pausanias' messengers began to be afraid, and their fear increased as the men who had not yet been sent realized that

73

none of those sent previously had ever returned home. So when Pausanias was recalled a second time and returned to Sparta, and when he was formally charged with crimes and sent messengers to tell the King, the last of the messengers to be sent was all the more afraid. He thought about the prospect of being killed, and not wanting to give in to his fear before knowing for sure, he copied Pausanias' seal, so that if his suspicions were wrong, he could use it again to reseal the letter. He opened the letter and read all the news about the planned enslavement of Greece; at the very end, he read the order for his own murder, so he brought the letter and showed it to the Spartan magistrates.

They had managed to collect evidence against Pausanias both in letters and in other reports, and they put their best efforts into learning the whole unadorned truth. They brought the messenger to Taenarus and made him sit there as a suppliant, secretly sending along with him some of their men. When Pausanias arrived, he asked the man whom he had sent as a messenger to Asia why he had come there as a suppliant. The man immediately called on Pausanias as a witness that he had done nothing that could justify the death penalty, and he confronted Pausanias with the fact that he had ordered him to be killed. He said that the enslavement of Greece meant little to him (since he wasn't even clearly free in his current situation), and he asked that first of all he should be given his freedom. Pausanias reassured him that he wouldn't be killed, asked him to keep quiet about what he knew, raised the suppliant up, and returned to Sparta; but the magistrates' men, who had heard every word, followed him. When all the magistrates learned the facts, they rushed out to arrest him, but as soon as they did, Pausanias eluded them by running into the temple of Athena of the Bronze House (*Athena Chalkioikos*), and sat down in supplication in one of the buildings inside the holy precinct. So they walled up the entrance, took off the roof of that building, and left him, sitting there as a suppliant, to die of thirst and starvation. And when they realized he was dying, they brought him out of the precinct and argued amongst themselves whether or not to bury him.

So, Alcetas, this was how Pausanias' good luck finally ended, and I've told you the whole story of the Spartan messenger boy. So don't mourn my exile any more. I'm indeed three times fortunate since however much envy was measured out for me, I managed to handle it equally well. But I can only blame my virtue for current circumstances, including the termination of the good services I used to provide in the context of democracy. But if at any time you hear that they are experiencing pity and regret for my suffering, instead of envy, since I've been brought so low, make sure you tell me, Alcetas, and maybe I could believe even Autolocus when he writes such stuff.

17. Themistocles greets Nicias and Meleager

I've come to Corcyra, just as I had planned at the beginning of my voyage. The trip was uneventful, and we easily made up for the time lost earlier when we were detained at Cyllene. So I sent the ship back to you right away, as well as most of the slaves, to ensure that I wouldn't make any greater demands on you than I think appropriate for someone in my position of exile. But I don't know how the Corcyrans can justify their current behavior. They admit that they remember all the favors I did for them, and they're not denying at all that they owe me gratitude; but they insist that this isn't a good time for them to pay me back, since they are too weak to resist my pursuers. They don't think it's fair for all of them to face ruin because of a favor owed to a single man, and they don't want to risk being destroyed in exchange for offering me sanctuary. So they're sending me away with kind words, and I'm afraid that this is just the beginning of more wandering for me.

18. Themistocles greets Aristeides

The inequality of our fortunes had already done away with any bad feelings, and it was just weakness of character that made you continue to be hostile towards me in my exile. But you, Aristeides, have even gone beyond this gesture of goodwill, and you have decided to help me in my misfortune in ways I never could have anticipated; I really never expected that you would support me to this point. In these matters my appreciation of your kindness hasn't lessened one bit, even though you weren't strong enough to make things work out well for me in the end. I still feel happier about your willingness to act on my behalf than I would have felt if you had actually saved me, since you fought against the Athenians who were so hostile towards me. Concerning my present wandering in exile, which I undertook because it seemed the lesser of two evils, don't you agree that this was a good idea? Polygnotus also wrote back to me, and he suggested the same thing, advising me to flee as quickly as possible, as if my sentence of punishment had already been approved. I suspect he's right, that I would have been punished if I had stayed.

For the Athenians wanted to bring me before the joint court of the Greeks, where the Dorians have the majority over the Ionians. And the majority was clearly going to be opposed to my case, while the minority was useless, so the entire situation was obviously going to be a disaster. Therefore it seemed to me that any other race of men, whether barbarian or Greek, would be more willing to give me sanctuary, and that the crimes I'm accused of might seem to be advantages in their eyes.

19. *Themistocles greets Antagoras*

Both of you, Antagoras and Autolycus, have often promised that you could easily correct the situation of my ostracism. You said that you would fight against my enemy Aristeides, that you would convince the people of Athens to vote against what he had voted for, and that already they thought less of him because he wasn't willing to let go of his hatred of me. But Aristeides has turned into more of a friend in need than both Antagoras and Autolycus. I wouldn't have experienced any of this horror, that which is still to come and that which I've already experienced, if three or four of my Athenian friends, including you, had decided to be as helpful as my enemy Aristeides was, or if you had even bothered to pay attention to my enemy's suggestions. But now, Antagoras, whose fault is it that I'm in exile: someone else's or yours? I don't think it's my enemies' fault that I'm not receiving an invitation to return home. But you've won, my friends, and I won't blame anyone at all in my exile, even if I'm going to suffer horribly.

20. *Themistocles greets Polygnotus*

Here's what happened to me, Polygnotus, after I fled Argos. You asked for it in writing, so I've written to you. After the messenger arrived in great haste, the one you sent to tell me the news and to urge me to flee, I immediately set forth from Argos, along with my friends Nicias and Meleager, and went to Cyllene, the Elean port city. There, because of a storm, I was almost caught by my pursuers. For as we started to sail to Corcyra (I had once done a favor to the Corcyraeans), we were held back for three whole days, and it looked as if our escape could no longer be kept hidden from the Spartans. On the fourth day, however, we had excellent sailing weather. So I thanked my friends and released them from their obligation (although they offered to accompany me even further), and, departing on the ship they had arranged for me, I had a smooth voyage to Corcyra. But it turned out that the Corcyraeans preferred to be safe rather than grateful, and when they were asked to pay back in turn my favor to them, they asked me not to break my journey in Corcyra. So I had no idea what to do next, because I'd already sent the ship back to my Argive friends, and I had fewer servants left with me than the number I had let go. But when the Corcyreans started talking tough, and it seemed more likely that they would hand me over to the authorities rather than defend me, I decided to sail to Gelon in Sicily.

Gelon was at that time the sole ruler of the Syracusans; he knew me very well, and he wasn't going to feel threatened by the Athenians. I found a ship belonging to men from Leucas, and on the next day I planned to set out for Italy. But a new message made me change my mind. Apparently Gelon had recently died, and his brother Hieron, who had just taken over the position of ruler, was dealing with a great deal of political confusion. So in the same ship, since I already had arranged it, I sailed off to Epirus, where I disembarked in the land of the Molossians and sat down in supplication at the hearth of Admetus. Admetus was at that time ruling the Molossian people; he thought that his kingship had prospered because of his piety, and so it was pretty obvious that he wouldn't ignore my supplication. Those who had been sent from Athens and Sparta to arrest me wherever they found me, using force if necessary, arrived by boat in the land of the Molossians the day after I did. They were very pleased to have caught me there, and proposed to take me away; so they approached Admetus and said the following:

> You didn't realize, Admetus, that you harbored a traitor in your home and at your hearth; in fact he betrayed you and the Molossians no less than he betrayed us. If he had succeeded in his plans, Admetus, we would have become suppliants at the Persians' hearth, and he might have become the king of the Thesprotians instead of you. Now do you still think we were unjust in our treatment of Pausanias, who has been punished for the same plotting? This man expects to be saved, and is trying to make you an accessory to his crime, but not even Athena of the Bronze Temple protected Pausanias. So tell this man get up; let him stop plotting and polluting your hearth. Let the Athenians and the Spartans be your allies instead of this single man, a traitor and a fugitive.

I was going to respond to their speech with some words that I thought would embarrass them and get them to go away, but Admetus spoke first:

> Men of Athens and Sparta, this particular situation alone will determine my response to Themistocles's supplication. If it were a case of deciding on the charge of treason, which I really shouldn't do in the first place since I'm neither an Athenian nor a Spartan, I would judge in Themistocles' favor. I should have thought that the sea battles at Artemisium and Salamis demand this verdict, and that Pausanias' treachery, even though you might want Themistocles to share in it, will always belong to Pausanias alone. You thought that I did not know this, and that my decision about Themistocles' supplication was due to my ignorance. This man hugs my hearth, fearing men but relying on the gods in Epirus; I will protect him as a suppliant and keep him from harm. I know I can't avoid the consequence of some men wanting to punish me for this, but I also admit that I fear the gods, and I believe that the protection of a suppliant is dearer to the gods than any amount of sacrifices.

Thus my accusers were disappointed, and left the territory of the Molossians.

Admetus then sent me to Macedonia, and when I arrived in Pydna, I visited Alexander, the ruler of the Macedonians. Alexander in turn sent me down to the harbor, where I found a ship that was sailing to Ionia. I boarded the ship and traveled east. I was hoping to find out if I would be treated justly there, since the Persian king was well aware of all the evil deeds I had committed against him. But as we were sailing, the good weather we had counted on for the journey didn't last, and we encountered a bad storm. It wasn't so much that the storm itself annoyed me, but the fact that we were diverted to Naxos. The Athenians were at that time sacking Naxos and we were sailing directly towards their fighting force. I felt totally helpless, and was already thinking that my supplication had been useless and that I had taken up a disastrous plan of escape. I was an exile who had run straight into the hands of his pursuers, and I was just about to be captured without even a struggle by the Athenians. I didn't want to leave the ship, since I thought nobody on board knew who I was, and I was afraid to be recognized by the men fighting. But my fellow passengers became suspicious; they thought I was bad luck, an obstacle to the success of their voyage, and so they were planning to kick me off the ship. In this risky situation, Diopeithes, one of my fellow travelers, a man from Bargylia, who had frequently before observed me and seemed to be intrigued, looked at me now even more carefully, and decided conclusively that I was the person he thought I was. So he sidled up close to me and said very quietly so no one else could hear:

> Fate mistreats you miserably, Themistocles, if your life depends entirely on not being recognized as Themistocles. But I know who you are, and although you've worried that any recognition would be a disaster, perhaps I can save you. For I'm the man you rescued when I was on a business trip to Artemisium; I had a personal enemy, a man from Hestiaea, who thought I should be executed because he claimed I got my sailing orders from the Persian king. But you didn't believe that story, and you criticized them for their attack. You did this even though you hadn't ever received any benefit from me, nor did you expect to receive any in the future. You were actually the Persian king's main opposition leader, and you had done good deeds for other men. I had given up the idea of repaying you, Themistocles, for that good deed and wasn't thinking about it, since I didn't expect that you would ever be in a situation where you would need me.

"My friend," I answered, "I don't consider what's happened now to be misfortune if I find myself at a point where I can get a repayment from you that will help me. I must thank you and wish you good fortune if indeed you have the power to save Themistocles." Right away he brought to me the captain of the ship who happened to be a friend of his. Filling him in on the situation, he asked him to take the ship as quickly as possible away from Naxos. The captain was not happy about this, and wanted to go right away to inform the Athenian squadron. I didn't need to beg him not to; I just threatened to tell the Athenians that he had rescued me from Greece in full knowledge of my identity and motivated by a bribe. At that the man was frightened and changed his mind, but insisted on a reward for his services. So I promised him a reward, and that night we weighed anchor and sailed to Ephesus. Once we got there, I found some Persian officials who had been sent by Artabazus to supervise Caria. I was no longer afraid to disclose my identity to Xerxes, so I

told them my name and said that I had come to help the house of
the Persian king. They reported my words to Artabazus, and took
me to Phrygia, since that was where Artabazus was posted. When he
heard my whole story, including the fact that I was determined
to make my way to the King, he encouraged me and sent me off
immediately, presenting me with two horses and an equal number
of servants, as well as thirteen other Persians who were supposed to
take care of the details of the trip and supplies; they used camels
for transport.

On my journey I passed a few mountains and a low valley; I
observed and traversed some large, completely flat plains which
I couldn't help admiring. Most of the area was inhabited and culti-
vated, but the desolate parts supported wild animals and flocks of
domestic stock. I also navigated many rivers and met up with various
groups of people. And soon, from my meetings with people, I began
to learn the elements of the Persian language, and as I got used to
it, the traveling was no longer so hard on me. When the journey
ended, we sought out the King, who'd been the object of our journey
all along. When a message was given to him that Themistocles the
Athenian was at his door, I was led into his presence; they placed
me right in front of his throne, and I stood there without any fear.
But he was clearly nervous as he looked me over, and said:

> Athenian stranger, there's already been a lot of gossip about
> you in my house; everyone is talking about you and the
> Persian disaster at Salamis. Please tell me how you have
> the audacity to be seen in my presence and to listen to my
> voice? Are you that same Themistocles who, according to
> the Persians, was the reason that both my father and I failed
> to conquer the Greeks? To have the Greeks in my power
> would be better for me than to punish you, but you have
> presented me with the latter possibility instead, so first we'll
> praise you and then we'll punish you.

When he had said this, it occurred to me in this difficult situation
that I would be justified in using a trick, excusable given the situation. Using this strategy, I spoke up:

> It's because I'm trying to escape punishment, King, that I've
> come to you as an ally. The Greeks were planning to punish
> me for helping your father. It was because of my goodwill
> toward you that I advised him to rush the expedition to

Salamis, at a time when the Greek force was divided, in disorder, and about to withdraw to the Peloponnese, thus offering a perfect opportunity for your attack. I blocked those who were eager to destroy the bridge, and specifically because of my actions your Persian soldiers were able to return home from Europe. And because of all this, I was about to be punished. I just barely managed to escape beforehand, so I could assist you and find a way of obtaining justice for my own case. Your power will ensure my success in this: I'll cause more trouble for the Greeks than I ever managed to cause for the Persians with their help.

The King answered: "When you deliver Greece to me, which I thought I'd lost because of your interference, you will rejoice and be showered with blessings. Let's put your words to the test of action."

From that point on, Polygnotus, I spent my time in the royal palace, where I was treated respectfully and continually asked questions about Greek affairs. The King himself, with whom I had many conversations in the Persian language, gave me a golden sword and a Persian garment woven of gold, and the members of the court also gave me presents as soon as he had started to do so. And now he thinks Artabazus is less reliable than I am, and he's sending me to the coast to take over his command. And he no longer grants me favors of fine clothing or gold, but the gifts now take the form of cities and entire lands. From his own imperial possessions, he split off Myus and Lampsacus and Magnesia on the Maeander, and handed them over to me. I gave Lampsacus its freedom and relieved that whole area of its full burden of taxation, and I earn income from Myus in Magnesia and Magnesia herself. I don't really enjoy my freedom or the money, but at least I have enough resources to make my exile bearable; my current wealth is greater than what any of you have the benefit of, my friends. But how could we, Greek men, be pleased by such abundance? So I've come to think of my present condition as a necessary evil rather than as a stroke of good luck.

Now, however, we've been overtaken by even worse luck: the King has remembered his campaign against the Greeks and is trying to get it started up again. This news has been delivered to me twice already. Is he proposing to put me at the head of his army, and to have the Persians serve under Themistocles? Am I supposed to fight against Athena and to do battle with the man in charge of the Athenian fleet? Many other things will come about, but this? Never!

81

21. *Themistocles greets Temenidas*

Please send me your four biggest silver wine jars and gold incense holders, the ones that have ancient Assyrian letters inscribed on them (*not* in the script that Darius, father of Xerxes, recently introduced for the Persians). And also send me half that number of iron breast-plates, the ones you showed me that you got from Admetus. Don't delay, and please be careful; don't even think of shipping them from Corinth, but do send the shipment off as quickly as you can. Give the stuff to the most trustworthy messengers you can find, and put it all in a boat sailing from any harbor as long as it isn't Cenchreae [Corinth's harbor]. Farewell.

"Chion of Heraclea"

1. *Chion to his father Matris*

Lysis brought me your letter on the third day of my stay near Byzantium; you and the whole family seem really worried about me. Someone else might offer comforting words and list at length the potential good that could come from my trip abroad, and even tell you to cheer up instead of being so sad. But here's what I want to say to you: imagine a prize for the virtue you hope to find in me. The prize should be that I make you happy parents, not that my education will cheer you up or make you happy, since you are so sad. It's better to set up bigger prizes for me, as if I were a winning athlete, so I can become a stronger competitor for them. So take my advice, father, and console my mother; she needs consoling and you should be the one to do it.

2. *Chion to his father Matris*

Thrason is travelling on business to Pontus, and he strikes me as a professionally useful man. I'm grateful to him for a favor he did me during my stay in Byzantium. When I wanted to go sightseeing in the area, he offered to be my tour guide and took good care of me, making sure that the trip wouldn't be too difficult for us, as if we were out hunting; it turned out to be much more luxurious, thanks to carriages and other equipment. Since he's now sailing to you, I thought I should send along this letter of recommendation, so he can be equally well treated by you. I don't think he'll want to do any sightseeing, since he's spent a lot of time on military duty in

Pontus, but I'm sure you'll receive him kindly into your home, just as you always do. I'm now itching to sail, but the winds aren't cooperating.

3. Chion to his father Matris

I'm very grateful to the winds that held me back and forced me to stay in Byzantium, even though at first I was frustrated and desperate to get going. But a good reason for staying even longer was the appearance of Xenophon, the disciple of Socrates. Xenophon is one of the Greeks who fought against Artaxerxes; he's an ally of Cyrus. And at first he followed one of the generals, not at all bothered by the rank of common soldier, even though Cyrus held him in great honor. But when Cyrus died in the first battle and the Greek generals had their heads cut off in violation of the treaty, he was chosen to be general, because of his bravery and other talents; he seemed the man most capable of rescuing the Greeks. And he didn't disappoint people's hopes, but led his small army through the middle of enemy territory to safety, camping each day near the king's generals.

Now all this is amazing, but even more amazing and important is what I later witnessed with my very own eyes. The Greeks were suffering from a long and harsh campaign; all they had achieved for their troubles was their own safety. So when the Byzantines received them with fear, they decided to sack the city. The Byzantines naturally became terribly anxious. When the invaders armed themselves and the trumpeter blew the signal, I grabbed my shield and spear and ran to the wall, where I saw some young men standing together. There was no real point in guarding the wall, since the enemy held the city already, but still we thought it would be easier to defend ourselves in a strategic location where we might survive a bit longer.

In the middle of all this, with the Greeks in disarray, we saw a man—long-haired, beautiful, serene—passing through the troops and curbing each man's violent impulses. This was Xenophon. When in response the soldiers urged him to give in to their larger numbers and let them put an end to their miserable wandering, he said "Come to order and make a plan; this crisis won't disappear while we're debating." Since they were ashamed not to obey him, they let Xenophon advance into the middle where he gave an amazing speech, as was evident from its results—of course we couldn't hear clearly what he said. The same soldiers who just a short while before had decided to sack the city were now calmly strolling in the marketplace to buy provisions, just like regular citizens instead of a cruel and angry mob.

This was a display of Xenophon's personality, his brains and eloquence. I certainly didn't wait around quietly for the man to leave, especially since, like the Byzantines, I had been saved by him (thanks to the winds I, too, was one of those about to be attacked), but I introduced myself to him. And he remembered your friendship with Socrates and encouraged me to study philosophy. On other topics, too, he spoke not like a soldier, by Zeus, but like a very enlightened man. He's now leading the army to Thrace. Seuthes, the king of Thrace, who is fighting with some neighbors, sent for him, promising his men full pay, and they have agreed to go, because they don't want to disband without money; they want to get something for their efforts, as long as they are still officially an army.

So you should know that I'm now much more eager to sail to Athens to study philosophy. Surely you remember that you used to urge me all the time toward philosophy, describing to me in a marvelous way the men who studied each of its disciplines seriously. For the most part you persuaded me, but I was very worried about one point in particular. I believed philosophy made men more serious in most of the matters it touched upon (for I thought that men achieved sound minds and a sense of justice only from philosophy), but that it severely damaged the practical side of their personalities and weakened them so that they turned to a quiet life. Peace and tranquility, as you used to say to me, were popular topics of praise by the philosophers.

So it seemed terrible to me, even if by studying philosophy I became better in some ways, that I would never be able to be brave, or become a soldier, or a hero, if it were necessary, but that I would abandon all that, enchanted by philosophy as if by some spell that would make me forget splendid deeds of action. I didn't know that even in the area of bravery, philosophers are better men, but I just learned this from Xenophon, not when he spoke to me about it, but when he himself showed what sort of a man he is. Although he often took part in conversations with Socrates, he is also strong enough to save armies and cities. In no way did philosophy make him less useful to himself or to his friends.

A quiet life is probably more conducive to happiness. A man who can live quietly will do well in all aspects of his life; whoever masters greed, desire, and other passions which defeat even those who conquer their enemies, is better off than a man who fights wars. So I hope by studying philosophy to become a better man all around—maybe not less brave, but certainly less rash. But now I've talked not just more than enough, but much more. You should know that I'm sailing soon, now that the winds are favorable.

4. *Chion to his father Matris*

I happened to meet Simus and his men as they were sailing in your direction on business, so I decided to report my adventures in Perinthus. The constellation of the Kids was just setting in the evening sky, so I advised my crew to delay our departure, especially since we could stay a while longer in Byzantium, but they didn't listen to me. Even worse, they made fun of my prediction, saying I'd been struck down by the sickness of astronomy, infected by the astronomer Archedemus. And I resisted them for some time, but then gave up, defeated. In all honesty, I didn't really know whether my predictions would come true, and when a fair wind and the promise of a safe trip appeared, it made me doubt my predictions all the more.

So we set sail, and they made fun of what I'd predicted until we passed by Selymbria, while I prayed that they should keep on joking until we disembarked. But when we came within about thirty stades of our destination, a terrible storm overtook us. And for a long time we were in desperate straits, unable to bring the ship into harbor. Then, barely catching sight of Perinthus in the distance, we forced ourselves in that direction, turning into excellent rowers, since the sails couldn't stand up to the force of the wind. After some bad experiences—I'll skip over those—we landed at Perinthus in the middle of the night and promptly fell asleep, but yet another storm was waiting for us there, no less fierce than the one at sea. The Perinthians were at war with the Thracians, and since we were ignorant of all this, we had no idea, even though we had spent twelve days in Byzantium and should have known about it; so the barbarians' attack came as a complete surprise.

Well, we woke up and went to see the city—or so we thought: Heraclides, my friend Agathon, and I, followed by some slaves, Baetylus, Podarces, and brave Philo. We were unarmed, but the slaves each wore a dagger, and Philo also brought along a spear. We'd gone a short distance from the harbor when we saw a camp near the city and, even worse, three horsemen quite near us. Philo gave me the spear so that he could run more quickly, and fled back to the ship, but I, realizing I couldn't outrun a horse, wrapped my cloak around my arm and steadied the spear, waiting. The slaves had the same idea, and Heraclides and Agathon grabbed some stones and hid themselves behind us. Meanwhile the three Thracians advanced, but before they came within reach, each one threw his javelin, landing just in front of us. The horsemen then turned back as if they had finished the job, and rode back into camp. We picked up the javelins, returned to the ship, cast off the moorings, and set sail. Now we're in Chios, and we enjoyed favorable winds for the whole journey. Tell Archedemus that the Kids setting in the evening sky portend heavy storms not only at sea, but even heavier ones on land. You can use my adventures to share a joke with him.

5. Chion to Matris

We've arrived in Athens and talked with Plato, Socrates' disciple. He's a wise man in so many ways, and teaches his disciples that philosophy is not incompatible with action, but rather something that works in two ways, helpful both for the practical aspect of life and also for quiet contemplation. You wrote to me that your acquaintance with Socrates might be quite an advantage as I make friends with Plato, too. So you should know that he pays close attention to those who have been with Socrates even just for one day, and he befriends people who are most able to benefit from him. I'm eager not to lose Plato's friendship, but be one of those men he benefits, since he can do them some good. He says there's no less joy in making men good than in becoming good yourself. He offers benefits to those friends who can take advantage of them, and he himself benefits no less from those who benefit from him.

6. Chion to Matris

Phaedimus arrived with a container of salted fish, five big pots of honey, twenty jars of wine, and on top of that three silver talents. I praise his loyalty and acknowledge your thoughtfulness. Could you please send me the first harvest of our country crops, if they're ready to pick? Then I can use them to entertain my friends and trick Plato, who usually refuses gifts. I don't want money at all, especially now that I'm studying with Plato in Athens. It would be very odd if, having sailed to Greece to become less fond of material things, a love of money should now sail to me from Pontus. I would be happier if you sent things that reminded me of my homeland, not of wealth.

7. *Chion to Matris*

Archepolis is Lemnian by birth, or so he says, but he's also an ignorant and unscrupulous man, at odds with everyone, especially with himself. On top of that he's totally reckless, blurts out whatever he's thinking at that moment, and what he thinks is always really stupid. As far as I know his first job was as a controller in Lemnos; then he tried other jobs but didn't behave appropriately. He got the notion to try his hand at philosophy, so he sailed to Athens, where he irritated Plato and badmouthed me. We seemed useless to him, since our conversations were about virtue, not money.

Now he claims he's going to Pontus on business—not a bad idea, since that's the only profession that might suit him. But his unstable, fickle nature doesn't allow him even enough self-awareness to understand his limitations or talents. He's always floating in the clouds of fantasy. Conveniently forgetting how he badmouthed me, he came and asked me to write you on his behalf. I didn't want to treat him like a Bellerophon, even if he is a wretch, so I gave him a letter as he requested, but handed another letter—this one—to Lysis, who will bring it to you.

I think you should welcome the man with complete friendliness and then say just before he leaves "This is the way Chion rewards those who have badmouthed him. This is one of the lessons he has learned, which you scoff at, namely not to defend himself against an evil person unless he himself can remain good." And I will remain good if I pay back evil men with good deeds. Of course I know that he won't be convinced, since his mind is impenetrably stupid, but even so I want you to follow this plan as a favor to me. I've told you these things about him frankly and without hiding anything, but I don't want to criticize him to anyone else. I'm telling you my opinion simply and clearly, not wrapped up in fancy words.

8. *Chion to Matris*

The man delivering this letter to you is Archepolis of Lemnos, going to Pontus on business. He asked for an introduction to you, and I gladly consented. He isn't exactly my friend, but here's a good opportunity to turn an acquaintance into a friend. You can share my opportunity by receiving him kindly. I am sure he's also an honest businessman, since he studied philosophy before turning to business.

9. *Chion to his friend Bion*

I wouldn't have expected you to neglect me so, nor do I want to interpret it in that way, but I wonder what's going on; no letter has arrived from you, even though piles of letters keep coming from my other friends. Whatever has happened up to now I can invent excuses for, but for the future, if the messengers are at fault, try to write more frequently—that way at least some of your letters will arrive safely. But if you just haven't been writing, do something about it—that's easy to fix. Surely our friendship is strong enough that we can resolve this problem. Don't tell me you've forgotten our school days: the Heraeum gymnasium on the banks of the Callichorus River, Callisthenes' lectures, and all our friends, how we shared our most private thoughts. Or do you think I don't remember all this and have forgotten it now that I've tasted philosophy? It's not right for you to have such a low opinion of our friendship and to judge me so poorly. Write often, from one remembering our friendship to another who also remembers.

10. *Chion to Matris*

Plato's brothers have four granddaughters. The eldest married Speusippus, with a decent dowry of thirty minas sent to Plato by Dionysius. Thinking it a good opportunity, I added a talent to the sum. For a long time he refused my gift, but I finally forced him to give in to my sincere and honest argument, saying,

> I'm sending you this gift not to make you wealthy, but for friendship's sake, and you should take it in that spirit. These gifts bring honor, unlike others, which disgrace the receiver; you honor friendship, but you don't respect wealth. You've already married off the other girls to very noble Athenians, but although they're wealthy, Speusippus, also a very noble young man, is poor.

I wanted to tell you about this good deed, since I don't know if anything better than this will ever happen to me in my whole life.

11. *Chion to Matris*

Bianor just handed me a letter in which you order me to return home. You implied that five years were sufficient for travel abroad, but that a sixth year would imply I had taken on resident alien status. You all know well how much I miss you and my hometown. But it seems to me that precisely this emotion forces me to spend more time in Athens. I want to be more useful to my friends, and only philosophy can teach me how to do this. A five-year stay seems insufficient not just for studying philosophy, but even for efficient businessmen to learn their job. Yet they prepare themselves for a worthless lifestyle, while we purchase virtue, which is paid for by native ability, hard work, and time—the first two items I'm not totally missing, but I do need time. I want to spend another five years here and then return, god willing. When you sent me away before, you found reason to be patient; use those same reasons now to resist grieving at my longer absence, and remember that it isn't just sailing off to the Academy that makes men good, but long and serious studying there.

12. Chion to Matris

I wrote to you earlier that I wanted to stay ten years here and then return home to Heraclea. But now that I've heard about the tyrant Clearchus who has come to power, I can't stand being safer than my fellow citizens, so I'll sail when spring comes, god willing—now in the middle of winter it's impossible. It would be really ridiculous if I were like those people who run away whenever something disturbs their city. It's really just the opposite—I want to be there when men of action are needed. Even if the help offered is totally useless, at least being willing to share your trouble seems to approximate virtue, even if the favor lacks a bit in effect. I have written this in confidence to you, since Lysis carries this letter.

13. Chion to Matris

You were right when you wrote that Clearchus doesn't fear Silenus, who captured his garrison, as much as me, a mere philosophy student. He didn't send men to attack him, at least not yet as far as I know, but against me he sent Thracian Cotys, one of his bodyguards—as I learned later. This assault happened just after I wrote about my illness—I'd already regained my strength sufficiently by then. I was wandering alone in the Odeum around noon, pondering some philosophical problem, when he suddenly attacked me. I understood the situation immediately. When I saw him grimly reach for his blade, I scared him with a loud shout and ran up to him, catching his right hand that already held the dagger. Then I kicked him, bent his arm back, and threw away his knife. I hurt my foot when he was knocked down, but not badly. After that he was dizzy, but I tied him up with his own belt with his hands behind his back, and took him to the magistrates. So he paid the price for his crime, and I, not at all intimidated, am ready to sail, but can't until the northwest winds stop blowing. It wouldn't be right for me to live freely here while my own city is under a tyrant's rule.

As far as my affairs are concerned, I still stand firm as before. I will be good, whether living or dying. So that I can fight on behalf of my city, you should persuade Clearchus that I long for peace and quiet, that I'm just a humble philosopher, and that my mind is completely apolitical. Ask Nymphis to persuade him too, since he is a friend of ours but also a relative of Clearchus'—that way he may be less suspicious. I write to you very openly, since I'm sending these letters through trustworthy men, and Clearchus, as you kindly told me, doesn't concern himself at all with our mail.

14. Chion to Matris

I arrived safely in Byzantium after a risky but quick sailing and have decided to stay for a while, as long as it seems appropriate, and send you my slave Crobylus to arrange a way for me to return and help my city. For our safety doesn't depend just on Clearchus. Now that things have come this far, I want to state my opinion clearly. I think the greatest danger for our city lies in our present misfortune. For now, as I see it, we face bloodshed and exile, deprived of our best citizens, enslaved by impious men; and from now on an even greater danger threatens the city. Inspired by this man's success, some men will wish to become tyrants, others will grow accustomed to slavery, and finally the city's affairs will collapse into permanent despotism. For small imbalances mark the beginning of lengthy and unceasing evils, just like diseases in the human body. Just as a person's disease is easily cured in the early stages, but as it gains strength it becomes difficult or even impossible to cure, so it goes with diseases of the citizen body: as long as the memory of freedom retains its strength and occupies the minds of the enslaved, people resist strongly. But once evil wins out and people stop talking about how to extricate themselves from it and discuss instead how to coexist most easily with evil, then we're utterly lost.

These are the evils and dangers our city finds itself in, but as for my own situation, I'm quite safe. In my opinion, only that which controls the mind along with the body can be called slavery. If it controls the body alone, without touching the mind at all, I don't think it can be called slavery. Here is my reasoning: if there is evil in slavery, this evil damages the mind—otherwise it shouldn't be called evil. For the fear of suffering and the pain that follows suffering are most terrible things only to those who aren't free. You ask me why? Can someone be a slave who's neither afraid of future evil nor bothered by present evil? How can he be a slave if he isn't touched by the evils of slavery? You should know that by studying philosophy, I have become someone Clearchus can never enslave, even if he ties me up and does his worst; he will never subdue my mind, which determines the condition of slavery or freedom. The body, after all, is a victim of circumstances, even when it isn't under the thumb of a tyrant. If he kills me, he will favor me with freedom in its purest form. For if the body surrounding the mind can't be reconciled with its own slavery, do you think that once separated from the body, the mind will fail to manage itself well? Not only am I a free man, whatever I suffer, but also Clearchus, whatever he imposes on me, will remain a slave, because he will act out of fear, and fear cancels out the mind's freedom.

So if you consider my situation, you'll see that it's safer for me to suffer than for Clearchus to act—no need at all to worry about me. To think first about such things is the mark of a man not entirely free. But my connection to my own city doesn't allow me this independence and freedom; instead it forces me to be involved politically and to confront danger, a danger not that I might suffer something myself, but that I might not be able to help my city in its distress. For this reason I have to plan ahead—even though I'm not afraid of death—so that I won't die before I can die for my city. Talk with the tyrant as I have suggested in previous letters, persuading him that we're peace-loving men, and write to me if anything else comes to mind about the political situation there. In order to save my city's freedom I have to sacrifice some of my own, as I think hard about these things and make plans.

15. Chion to Matris

I rejoice along with my city that the tyrant has been fooled by what you said about me. I'll write to him too, as you recommend, leading him as far away from the truth as possible. If I told the truth, I would disappoint the hopes of my fellow citizens and friends, and they don't deserve to be cheated like that. I've come to the conclusion that it's in a city's best interest for a tyrant to be utterly cruel, rather than for him to curry favor with the masses and pretend to be moderate. Let me explain: cruel men are quickly destroyed, and even if they aren't removed from power, they still make people hate tyranny and make despotism look completely wretched. Because of this, everyone becomes more cautious about the city's political future and thinks more about protecting democracy. But when a tyrant enslaves people and then curries favor with those he has enslaved, even if he is removed quickly, he still leaves behind evil traces of his power in each person's mind: some are convinced that they'll be rewarded, others are overwhelmed by his authority, and all become blind to the common good. And if he is removed from power, they sympathize with him as if he were indeed a moderate ruler, and they don't guard themselves against tyranny as a deadly evil; they don't understand that, even if a tyrant is mostly moderate, he must be destroyed simply because he has the power also to be cruel. Clearchus himself is savage and therefore easy to handle since he is hated, and he'll make it harder for others to establish a tyranny. If he'd pretended to be moderate, he would've enjoyed a good reputation and paved the way for others later who might wish to capture our citadel. But you know all this, of course. I'm glad that you think my plan is safe— my writing style and the delivery of my letters—and I'm also glad that you finally admit it's not such a bad idea. I'm enclosing a copy of the letter I sent to Clearchus; I made it extremely convoluted and enthusiastic, so that he might despise me as a harmless chatterbox.

16. Chion to Clearchus

While I was in Athens studying philosophy, my father and some of our mutual friends wrote that you were suspicious of me, and they suggested that I defend myself against your accusations. I think this is a good idea—the proper thing for me to do. But while I'm sure they are right, I don't know what I am suspected of, and this ignorance makes any apology somewhat difficult. I wasn't there when you seized power, and since I was absent I was unable to speak up against anything; no word or action of mine has had any impact at all on the state of affairs over there. I haven't discovered what sorts of disagreements there might be across the sea between a powerful ruler and a man living abroad with just a small household, and since I haven't seen the actual accusation, I don't know how to shape my self-defense.

But I do know one thing: I have no plans that you should be nervous about, and in fact I can convince you that my mind is totally unreceptive to such plots. Even if I hadn't studied philosophy, the fact that you've never harmed me would be sufficient evidence that I don't hate you. For not even people unacquainted with philosophy, unless they are quite mad, make enemies for the fun of it, nor do they love or hate certain people as if it were a childish game (far from it); rather, they know very well that nothing is more distressing to men than hatred. When men disagree with one another because of some incurable wrong, only then do they hate one another, and even then unwillingly.

But until today, no act of hatred, whether large or small, has divided us. Yet you are full of suspicions and accusations, while my heart is pure. Why would I suddenly want to revolt against you, especially since I haven't yet seen my city under your rule? Or, by Zeus, do you think I've been made overconfident by the many warships and cavalry troops here in Athens, so that, if nothing else, you might suspect me of being able to be an enemy? I traveled abroad with eight slaves and two friends, Heraclides and Agathon, but I'm returning after losing two slaves from the household. I don't see how anyone can persuade you that this is a sufficient force against you. And you aren't taking this into account, that if I became aware that I was justly under suspicion, I would never willingly put myself into the hands of the man suspecting me. Or am I so in love with the feeling of hatred that I don't try to sustain friendships, but willingly deliver my body into the hands of one who will punish it justly? But this apology is sufficient even for those who aren't philosophers, and indeed more than sufficient.

So, I wasn't entirely unfit for appreciating the benefits of philosophy, and I added my own efforts to my natural talents as best I could. As a young man I wasn't ambitious for positions of power or great honors, but prayed simply to become an observer of nature. And this desire led me to Athens and made me Plato's friend, and even now I haven't had my fill of him. I had such a natural inclination towards peace and quiet that even as a youth I utterly despised anything that could lead to a busy life; after moving to Athens, I didn't go hunting, refused to sail with the Athenians off to the Hellespont against the Spartans, and avoided lessons that might have made me hostile towards tyrants and kings. Instead I conversed with a man who loved peace, and studied very reverent ideas. The first thing he taught me was to wish for peace. He claimed that peace was the guiding light of philosophy, whereas politics and officiousness obscure it in darkness, and make it very hard to find for those who seek it.

But since I seemed by nature well suited for philosophy, although not easily convinced of its principles, I spent my time studying about god, the all-seeing one, and the arrangement of the universe; contemplating the laws of nature, I learned to honor justice and all the other things philosophy teaches. For nothing is more worthwhile than philosophy—not just understanding it but also the whole process of philosophical investigation. What could be better for a man, since his mortal nature is mixed in with a bit of the divine, than to spend his free time just with his immortal parts, and to bring these parts closer to that which is related to them? For I believe that a man's godlike parts are related to the divine.

This is the kind of thing I craved and was eager to learn, but as for politics, if you pardon my speaking freely, I didn't consider it worth my attention. But I've learned many sorts of things, some of which I can now apply to our situation. I learned to honor a man who does no wrong, and that it's best to repay an unjust man with good deeds—but if this isn't possible, then to repay him with quiet inaction. I also learned to consider a friend the most valuable possession, to avoid making enemies for myself, and if I do have an enemy, to try to make him my friend instead. Finally, I learned never to get so upset about something evil that it could disturb my mind and distract me from my own affairs. So why have you decided to treat me like a conspirator when I know these things? Please don't. You keep the job of war and politics, but reserve for me just enough space in your city that's appropriate for a peaceful man leading a quiet life. If you let me speak with my friends, I'm sure I can soften them up and make them lose interest in politics, if that's what you want, by reciting praises of our practice of peaceful inactivity, since if I were thinking otherwise, I would be very ungrateful.

Well what if I were distressed and distracted as you suspect, and the gentle goddess of Tranquility appeared before me and spoke these words:

> Chion, you ungrateful wretch, don't you remember those beautiful lessons you learned, or even your true self? When I was around you practiced justice, acquired self-control, and turned your mind toward god; you reaffirmed your connection to him, and despised those base things that seem marvelous to other people: ambition, wealth, and similar things. So now, you ought to be grateful, spending time with me in conversation, ruled by a higher law and revealing

a stronger intellect, but instead you plan to abandon me,
forgetting all the things you learned from philosophy,
including the rule that you should investigate thoroughly
what you don't yet know. So how are you going to investigate or find out things without me?

If she said these things, how could I answer her properly? I don't see
any way.

You should know that I'm always talking to myself like this
(most men talk to themselves as they think aloud), and I wouldn't
want to be deprived of these things. Rest assured that you have
nothing to fear from me. For my peaceful inactivity will not be
affected by your worldly affairs.

17. Chion to Plato

Two days before the festival of Dionysus I will send you my most
loyal slaves, Pylades and Philocalus. I've made great efforts for a long
time now to avoid any suspicion, but at the festival I'm going to
attack the tyrant. On that day he's leading a procession in honor
of Dionysus, so I think he'll have a smaller number of bodyguards.
And even if this isn't the case, even if I have to go through fire, I
won't hesitate, and I won't dishonor myself or your philosophy.
We're a strong group of conspirators, stronger in loyalty than in
numbers. I know that I'll be killed, but I pray that this will happen
only after I finish the job of killing the tyrant. If I die after releasing
my fellow citizens from tyranny, then I will leave this life happy,
singing a hymn to Apollo and carrying off the prize of victory.

All the evidence—sacrifices, bird omens, my own skill in
prophecy—points to my accomplishing this deed successfully. And
I myself have seen a vision, clearer than in a dream. A woman
appeared to me, a divinely beautiful and tall creature, who seemed
to crown me with wild olive branches and headbands; then she
showed me a lovely tomb and said: "Now that you have worked
hard, Chion, enter this tomb and take a rest." Because of this vision,
I have high hopes of dying a noble death, for I believe that there is
nothing deceitful in the oracles of one's mind, and I know you
think the same. If the prophecy comes true, I think I'll be happier
than I would be if I lived into old age after killing the tyrant. Once
I've accomplished my great deed, it's better for me to leave the
world before enjoying any more time here. Whatever I do will be

considered much greater than whatever I suffer, and I myself will be more honored by the men I help if I buy freedom for them with my own death. It looks better, and those who profit from the deed think it is better, if the person who performs the deed doesn't benefit from it himself. So I'm actually very cheerful, even facing a prophecy of death. Farewell, Plato, and I hope you live happily into a ripe old age. I'm sure I speak to you now for the last time.

5

PSEUDO-HISTORICAL LETTER COLLECTIONS OF THE SECOND SOPHISTIC

INTRODUCTION

Pseudonymous letters, also called pseudo-historical or pseudepigraphic, are unique to the period of the Second Sophistic. They are letters written by an anonymous writer in the voice of a famous person, either mythical or historical (Speyer 1971). We have already encountered one example of this in the novella *Chion of Heraclea*. Later we will see how Alciphron further developed the idea behind such false letter writing by inventing a series of pseudonymous correspondences, some between wholly fictional writers and addressees, others between courtesans and their lovers, including Menander and Epicurus, well known public figures in fourth-century Athens. But the subset of pseudonymous letters collected in this section is attached to such famous historical figures as Socrates, Plato, and Demosthenes, and thus logically termed pseudo-historical.

The most important shared trait of pseudo-historical letters, beyond their composition sometime in the Second Sophistic, is their supposed historicity: they represent scenes from the lives of famous persons from Greek history through those persons' letters. The protagonists explore their feelings, thoughts, and experiences in letters, sometimes revealing inner development as in a *Bildungsroman* (e.g. Chion, Hippocrates), but at other times reflecting the confusion of current events (e.g. Themistocles). The anonymous writers aim for accuracy in all areas—dialect, perspective, setting—but often, in their attempt at realism, provide so many specifics that they trip themselves up on anachronisms, and reveal their fictional nature.

This type of writing has its roots in the rhetorical character sketches (*ethopoieia*) mentioned previously. By the Roman imperial period, the imaginative composition of letters to and from famous men was a standard component of rhetoric (Russell 1983: 1–20; Speyer 1971: 32–3). These literary exercises in turn grew beyond the schoolroom into the form of public declamations on fictional topics, both judicial and historical (Bowie 1970: 5). Thus it must have been a slippery slope between real and fictional "documents" for those with any creative tendencies. Benefiting from such training, writers developed even more sophisticated patterns of impersonation: some invented the writings of a single correspondent (e.g. Chion's letters), while others imitated the voices of several writers within a related group (e.g. the Socratic letters). Pseudonymous epistolographers could work the bare bones of any biography into a compelling life story. They were at once scholar and artist, researching historical materials for the basic facts, and then using their imagination to elaborate creatively and dramatically on those facts. Interestingly, most of the collections turn out to be the product of more than one author, quite possibly reflecting an accretion of invented letters around an original, in some cases (e.g. Plato) even authentic, core.

The principal impulse behind the work of a pseudonymous letter writer may have been the desire to illuminate a figure from the glorious past through a more intimate character portrait than a standard biography would allow. The letter writer presents an "apology" for the hero's life, or challenges a later generation to admire his accomplishments, viewing historical events through the lens of one man's personal correspondence. The genre itself suggests an eagerness on the part of authors to supplement existing information with more colorful or human touches, and a related interest in unearthing evidence for early stages of certain philosophical "schools," as in the case of the Cynics' adoption of Anacharsis as their culture hero (Speyer 1971: 131–50). The urge to read the private words of remarkable people reveals a kind of antiquarian interest similar to our contemporary fascination with the diaries and private correspondence of former heads of state; thus we search Solon's letters, for example, for clues about his views on democracy that his public poetry might not reveal. The curious reader hopes to find in letters a "mirror of the soul," to use a phrase from one ancient epistolary theorist ("Demetrius" *On Style* 227). One could call our readings of such letters "voyeuristic," as we seek glimpses into the private thoughts of a public figure, not really caring whether what we discover is noble or base, as long as we find something new.

Letters in particular, more than any other narrative format, tempted ancient authors to experiment with pseudonymous composition. There was greater stylistic freedom and less artistic constraint in a letter, as it was meant to have been composed for a friend's eyes only, and not subject to literary or political scrutiny. All the writer had to do in order to succeed in his enterprise was to present a consistent characterization and keep within the bounds of bio-graphical accuracy and historical probability. The use of well known names, specific places, even precise dates was required if the anony-mous author wished the details of his letter to ring true, since the audience evaluated the work according to standards of verisimilitude and probability. When mismanaged, however, these attempts at historical accuracy allow later scholars to challenge the work's authenticity, as in the case of British classicist Richard Bentley's famous denunciation of the letters of Phalaris as forgeries (Hinz 2001; Bentley 1697). Bentley wrote his influential volume in 1697, arguing that the author of the *Letters of Phalaris*, as well as most of the authors translated below, were trying to pass the letters off as the genuine article, when in fact they were nothing but pale imitations from a later age. Bentley claimed that the pseudo-historical authors consciously intended to deceive their readers and that their works were thus worthless as historical documents. His condemnation of the whole genre led to a general neglect of this material over the next three centuries; even the great ancient historian Ronald Syme's statement that there need be no "criminal handiwork" at play, and that most literary impostures were created without serious intent to deceive, has done little to correct the situation (Syme 1972: 3–17). But these letters are very much worth reading in their own right as examples of how the classical past was received and reconstructed by its heirs in the Second Sophistic.

The only complete text of the pseudo-historical letters is still that of Rudolf Hercher's *Epistolographi Graeci* (Paris 1873). Most of the pseudo-historical letters collected within are written in the voices of philosophers (Aristotle, Democritus, Heraclitus, Hippocrates, Plato, the Pythagoreans, Socrates, the Socratics, Zeno), wise men (Anacharsis, Apollonius of Tyana, Crates, Diogenes, Solon, Thales), literary figures (Euripides, Lucian, Xenophon), orators (Aeschines, Demosthenes, Isocrates), and politicians or tyrants (Artaxerxes, Brutus, Dion, Periander, Phalaris, Themistocles). While the names are limited to men already famous from other texts and contexts, the actual types of letters written in their voices are quite varied. Some are familiar from taxonomies of letter writing: letters of consolation, invective, invitation, recommendation, request for payment of debt, diatribes, and didactic treatises. Others are personal letters about family affairs, propagandistic messages glorifying various causes, letters attempting to convert readers to a certain belief, and letters of narrative description. It is impossible here to discuss all the pseudo-historical collections in detail, so for the sake of brevity, the letters translated below have been chosen from three illustrative groups: philosophers, sages, and orators.

Private letters from a philosopher or a sage could be expected to offer insights into the wise man's mind, and if they were well-researched and true to the philosopher's teachings, the letters could provide additional material for the schools of thought he had established. We can see this principle at work in the letters of several philosophers (Plato, Heraclitus, the Cynics), but particularly in the case of the thirty-five letters attributed to **Socrates** and the **Socratic** disciples (Holzberg 1994: 188–9; Sykutris 1933). The writings of his followers, whether in his name or in their own voices after his death, praise Socrates' actions and beliefs, and transfer the oral tradition that developed around him into a more permanent written form. The letters contain little profound philosophical material, but they do create a fuller picture of the great man. The historian Xenophon followed a similar impulse in his biographical narrative of Socrates, but the epistolary form encourages a great deal more vividness and emotion, particularly when several voices speak consecutively. The selections below show the human side of Socrates; he comes across as full of conviction, but also a little bit impractical. In the first of seven letters supposedly written by Socrates himself, the great man defends his ascetic lifestyle and then asserts that his inheritance to his children will be not gold, but the far more valuable commodity of good friends. The next selection is from his disciple Aeschines, who is aware of his teacher's views but is also obviously a more practical man. He writes after Socrates' death to Socrates' wife Xanthippe, consoling her with philosophical commonplaces, but also promising financial assistance to her and her "baby birds." Aeschines' brief and responsible message to the widow contrasts nicely with Socrates' idealistic yet somewhat self-absorbed stance in his letters.

The plurality of voices in the Socratic collection contrasts with the single voice of **Plato**'s thirteen letters, among the most disputed texts of antiquity. Scholars debate whether to read all the letters as forgeries, because they are so alien to the thought and character of the philosopher Plato familiar from the dialogues, or, for the very same reason, to accept some of them as genuine (Wohl 1998; Gulley 1971). Many of the Platonic letters are addressed to tyrants, and they explore the idea of a mutually beneficial relationship between philosopher and tyrant. Plato offers advice and criticism in an attempt to turn the tyrant into a wise ruler, describing the ideal state in the possibly genuine seventh letter, where philosophers rule the cities and the former rulers have in turn become philosophers. The observations on contemporary politics, and the concern about proper government and the philosopher's civic duty in Plato's letters, may have influenced the author of *Chion of Heraclea*. But instead of this serious letter, which has already received much scholarly attention, I have chosen one of the less well-known but surely pseudonymous letters: a rather chatty message from Plato to the Syracusan tyrant Dionysius, whose court he had visited. It concerns itself more with bank accounts, gifts, and gossip than with pearls of wisdom, showing us a side of Plato that could only be revealed in a private letter to a friend.

The rest of the letter selections are admittedly arbitrary choices on my part, organized alphabetically by author, and generally accessible without too much commentary, so I will not say much in the way of introduction, and provide minimal bibliographical references. The letter of **Aeschines** describes the fourth-century BCE Athenian orator's misadventures with a particularly wild friend, Cimon, on a sightseeing trip to the Trojan ruins, where they crash a wedding party with hilarious results. Aeschines aptly mimics Homeric epic by claiming that even if he had "a hundred tongues and a hundred mouths" he couldn't possibly describe all of Cimon's shamelessness; but he gives it a good try anyway, and the resulting narrative is an erotic short story in epistolary form. Aeschines closes with "I thought I should write you a letter about it, since . . . I suspect you'll find my story worth at least a chuckle," reminding us that many of these letters are supposed to be read just for fun. The letters written in the voice of the sixth-century BCE Scythian sage **Anacharsis** may be dated somewhat earlier than many in this section, perhaps as early as the Hellenistic period (Kindstrand 1981; Reuters 1963). Anacharsis challenges the ethnocentric view that Athenian culture is superior to all others, and tries to convince various powerful men (Solon, Croesus) that even a barbarian can be wise. The letters from the second-century CE ascetic Neo-Pythagorean **Apollonius** of Tyana to the Stoic philosopher Euphrates are harsher in tone, full of blunt and sometimes downright rude advice from the sanctimonious wandering sage; his eighth letter is of particular interest, offering snappy responses to such apparently common criticisms as "Apollonius totally refuses to take a bath," or "He avoids all meat" (Penella 1979).

I have included two letters from orators other than Aeschines: **Demosthenes** defends himself to the Athenians against Theramenes' slander, getting in some effective digs against his opponent ("drunken insults" from a man "born in a whorehouse"); **Isocrates** addresses Timotheus, the son of Isocrates' former pupil Clearchus, tyrant of Heraclea, whom we met earlier in Chion's letters. The orator writes to Timotheus upon his accession to power in Heraclea (ca. 346 BCE), applauding his democratic leanings, renewing their friendship, and, in the manner of Polonius to Laertes, volunteering words of advice to the younger man. The remaining four selections are in the voices of wise men, presenting in letters the thoughts and idiosyncratic behaviors of the Cynics Diogenes, Democritus, and Hippocrates, the Athenian Solon, and the scientist Thales. **Diogenes** boasts of the simplicity of his lifestyle, throwing away his drinking cup after seeing a servant use his cupped hands for collecting water. The selections from **Hippocrates** and **Democritus** provide us with rare instances of a letter sequence (Rütten 1992; Smith 1990). First the people of Abdera in Thrace write a communal petition to the great doctor on the island of Cos, begging him to cure one of their most famous citizens, Democritus, of his apparent madness; Hippocrates writes back promising to come quickly, refuses any form of payment, and expresses the hope that they are mistaken about the man's condition. Then Democritus himself writes to Hippocrates, apparently after the doctor's visit, chiding him for listening to the foolish people of Abdera, and slyly referring to his own treatise on insanity which he has included in his parcel for Hippocrates' edification; Hippocrates writes back politely, glad to begin a correspondence with an intellectual equal, and returns the favor by sending Democritus his treatise on hellebore. One can easily imagine the subsequent letters flying fast and furious between Cos and Thrace.

The letters of Thales and Solon complete this section, both transmitted in Diogenes Laertius' third-century CE compendium of the life and times of famous ancient philosophers from Thales to Epicurus. **Thales**' first letter includes the information that he and Solon have already sailed to Crete and Egypt in their thirst for knowledge, and his second letter, addressed to Solon, invites his friend to settle with him in Miletus. **Solon** writes letters of advice to friends and rulers, including two tyrants, Periander and Pisistratus; he reminds them that he had the opportunity to become a tyrant himself, but will always choose democracy over tyranny. Finally, in two related letters, Solon appears predictably as a champion of democracy, but also as a wise and cautious statesman. To his friend Epimenides (*Letter 2*) he calls Pisistratus a flatterer and a destroyer of democracy who has enslaved the Athenian people; writing to Pisistratus himself (*Letter 3*), however, he slightly modifies his tone, writing that he is "willing to admit that [Pisistratus] is a fantastic tyrant," but, in a wonderfully diplomatic understatement, that "this isn't a good time for [Solon] to return to Athens."

The pseudo-historical letters satisfied their authors' urge to write biography, autobiography, and fiction all at once. For the most part, they begin where the "official" story leaves off, and provide details for their subjects' lives that, even if unsubstantiated by any other evidence, are often more enjoyable to read about than drier, factual versions. They must have been enjoyable to read, since so many letters survived from antiquity. This impulse to tell or read about the story of a great man from a different angle will eventually evolve in the modern world into different forms: the historical fiction of Tolstoy's *War and Peace*, for example, where the reader may well learn more about Russian social customs and imperial battle strategies than from any history textbook, or the popular contemporary genres of historical biography, official and unofficial, of celebrities as varied as Churchill and Ray Charles. But for the ancient Greeks, it was the letter that best suited revelations of a public man's private life.

PSEUDO-HISTORICAL LETTER COLLECTIONS OF THE SECOND SOPHISTIC: THE TEXTS

Aeschines

Letter 10

You can't imagine what that fellow Cimon made us go through in every town and harbor we visited, ignoring both laws and common decency. I had come to Troy, eager to see the place, including the infamous beach; but I'll keep quiet and won't write about what I saw there, since I think the topic's been done to death already. If I try to copy that fancy poetry stuff, I'm afraid I'll make a fool of myself. But as for Cimon's tricks, and his utter shamelessness, even if I had a hundred tongues and a hundred mouths, I wouldn't have the strength to describe it all.

After we spent several days at Troy and still hadn't had enough of gazing at the famous graves (my idea was to stay until I could see all the items mentioned in the epics and connected to the heroes), the day came when a host of Trojans were trying to arrange weddings for their daughters, at least those who were the right age. There were big crowds of girls getting ready to marry. It was customary in the region of Troy for brides-to-be to go to the river Scamander, wash themselves in its waters, and say this phrase out loud, as if it were something sacred: "Scamander, take my virginity." One of the girls who came to bathe at the river was Callirhoe; she was beautiful, but from a poor family. So we, together with their relatives and the rest of the crowd, were watching the festival and the girls bathing from a distance, as was appropriate for those who weren't immediate family members. But our fine fellow Cimon hides himself in a bush on the banks of the Scamander, and crowns his head with reeds; he was clearly prepared to snare poor Callirhoe, and the day provided the opportunity for his trap. I found out later that she was in the river pronouncing the customary phrase, "Scamander, take my virginity," when Cimon jumped out of the bushes in his Scamander costume and said, "with pleasure! Since I am Scamander, I take and accept Callirhoe, and promise to be good to you." As soon as he said this, he grabbed the girl and disappeared. But the incident didn't end there. Four days later there was a procession in honor of Aphrodite; the recently married girls participated, and we were spectators. When the new bride saw Cimon watching with me, acting for all the world as if he had done nothing wrong, she gestured toward him reverently, and turning to her chaperone, said, "Nurse, do you see Scamander there, to whom I gave my virginity?" When the nurse heard this, she gasped out loud, and the affair became public knowledge.

So I go back to my quarters, grab Cimon, and give him a piece of my mind, calling him wicked, saying that we're in big trouble now because of him. But he wasn't scared at all, or ashamed of what he'd done; he made it worse by rattling off a long list of people everywhere who had committed crimes that should have been punished by torture. He claimed the same thing had happened near the river Meander in Magnesia with one of the young men there, and that from that day on, the father of Attalus the athlete remained convinced that the boy wasn't his biological son, but Meander's; he thought that this explained Attalus' amazing muscles and physical strength. When the boy was finally beaten and threw in the towel, he left the games and said he thought the river was angry with him for failing to acknowledge Meander as his father before when he had been victorious. He might have been beaten in the games, but he

104

sure wasn't at a loss for an excuse! Similarly, near Epidamnus, Cimon claimed, a rather naive musician was convinced that his child, born from his wife's adulterous affair, was really Heracles' son.

"I didn't make any babies," Cimon said. "I just had one pleasant conversation with a luscious girl I saw bathing in the river, escorted by her old slave. Anyway, it seems to me that the events at Troy aren't wholly horrible and tragic; we should look at the funny side of it all, and stage *The Scamander Story* as a comedy!" And I, waiting only for him to stop his blaspheming, felt myself grow numb with disbelief at his outrageous behavior. But he seemed all set to embark on two more sexual adventures at the upcoming festivals of Apollo and Dionysus. Just then I noticed a mob heading toward our front door. "This is it," I said, "They're coming to get us." I ran straight out back and fled to Melanippides' house, and afterwards that evening to the shore and out to sea. But we were driven back to our host's house by a vicious wind that nobody would have dared to sail in unless he was trying to escape the Cimonian curse. After suffering all this, I thought I must write you a letter about it, since you've experienced far worse than me. I suspect you'll find my story worth at least a chuckle.

Anacharsis

Letters 1, 2, 9, 10

1. Anacharsis to the Athenians

You laugh at my accent because I can't pronounce Greek clearly. You Athenians think Anacharsis talks funny, but the Scythians think the Athenians are the ones with foreign accents. You should rank men not by their accents but by their opinions; besides, even the Greeks themselves speak with different accents. The Spartans don't speak an elegant Attic, but their deeds are brilliant and honorable. The Scythians don't criticize language that can resolve a crisis, and they don't praise language that's ineffective. And even you Athenians often go about your business without caring whether a man can speak correctly or not. You bring in Egyptian doctors, hire Phoenician ship captains, go shopping in the market without paying native Greek-speakers more than their products are worth. You have no qualms about buying from foreigners, as long as the price is right. Whenever the kings of Persia and their allies, proud as they are, want to speak to the Greek ambassadors in Greek, they have no choice but to speak badly, but you don't criticize their plans or their actions. You can't call their language bad if the intentions are good, or if good deeds result from the words. The Scythians judge a speech poor when its arguments are faulty. You'll miss out on a lot if you despise foreign accents and therefore don't understand what's being said. You'll be resistant to introducing things that might be useful for you. Why do you admire imported woven cloth but disapprove of foreign speech? You want flute-players and singers to sound in tune, yet you object to poets who compose in meter if they don't fill up their lines with Greek words. When people speak, you should pay attention to what's actually being said, because you might benefit from it. If you pay attention to foreigners, you won't encourage your wives and children to ignore you if you speak incorrectly. It's better to be rescued by obedient people who speak incorrectly than to be hurt badly by following people who speak elegant Attic Greek. Men of Athens, your attitude ranks you with the uneducated and the ignorant; no sensible person would think such things.

2. Anacharsis to Solon

The Greeks are wise, but no wiser than foreigners. The foreigners' gods granted them, too, the ability to know what's good. And it's possible, through careful examination, to check whether we think good thoughts, and to test whether our actions correspond to our words, and if we resemble those who live well. But don't let beautiful architecture and high fashion get in the way of correct judgment, since people beautify their bodies in different ways, all according to their native customs. The signs of stupidity are the same for foreigners and Greeks, as are the signs of intelligence. So Anacharsis came to your door, wanting to stay on as your guest; but you turned me away and told me I should look for hospitality in my own country. But if someone presented you with a Spartan dog, surely you wouldn't insist that he take that dog to Sparta and give it to you there. When will we ever be hosted by other people, if we all make the same argument? Solon, you're a wise Athenian, but this doesn't seem right to me. I'm tempted to travel again to your door, not expecting what I did before, but to find out what you think about this issue of hospitality.

9. Anacharsis to Croesus

The Greek poets in their verses divided up the universe among the sons of Cronus: one was assigned heaven, the other the sea, and the third the world below. This division comes from the Greeks' self-interest. Since they don't know how to cooperate themselves, they attribute their own bad manners to the gods. But they didn't include the earth in their calculations, and they let it be common property.

So let's consider where this train of thought leads us. The Greek poets wanted all the gods to be honored by men; they imagined them handing out good things and warding off evil. Long ago the earth was the common possession of men and gods. But after a while men acted improperly by taking what was common to all and establishing private precincts for the gods. In return, the gods gave men appropriate gifts: discord, desire, and mean spirits. As these qualities were mixed and separated, all the evils in the world came into existence for mortals: tilling, sowing, mining, and fighting. They brought in much more fruit than they harvested, and they tried various crafts but the luxury they found was short-lived. They searched for the earth's treasures in various ways and claimed it was a marvel when someone found something; they even considered the person who first discovered this little thing to be a most blessed man. Yet they're totally unaware that they deceive themselves, like little children. First they put no value on anything gained by hard work, but then they end up thinking the work itself is wonderful.

I've heard that the evil that falls upon most men has attacked you, too. Other evils will follow from this, since neither great wealth nor landownership can buy wisdom. People say that those whose bodies are filled up with mostly foreign things will also be filled with diseases. If you have any desire for good health, they say you should plan a quick escape. You have doctors for your excessively self-indulgent bodies, but none for your souls. You'd be wise to renounce indulgence. When big piles of gold flow in your direction, along with the gold comes its bad reputation, as well as the envy and greed of those who want to steal it from you. So if you'd purified yourself of the disease, you would've become healthy, speaking freely and ruling well. Because this is healthy for a king; if he acquires something good inside himself, it's no wonder if he's also good on the outside. But since you lack self-control, the disease caught hold of you, attacked you, and turned you into a slave instead of a free man. Don't despair—just think about the image of a fire that starts out in a forest: it turns to ashes whatever it burns and feeds off whatever isn't burned. So the evils that were yours in times past have migrated to those who possess you and your property. You can expect that those who come after you will experience misery, and here's a story I myself witnessed to prove it.

A big river called the Danube flows through the land of the Scythians. Some merchants on the river accidentally sailed their ship against a sunken rock, and when they realized they couldn't fix it, they went away in tears. Now some robbers sailed by with an empty ship; not understanding the merchants' problem, they eagerly loaded the cargo, immediately transferring the goods from the other ship to theirs, totally unaware of the accident about to happen. So the first ship, when it was emptied, became lighter and started to float again; but the ship that took on its cargo swiftly sank to the bottom of the river, as punishment for robbing someone else's property.

This is always the danger for someone who owns property. But the Scythians stand apart from all these things. We think the earth belongs to everyone. Whatever the earth chooses to give us, we take; but whatever it holds back, we let it keep. We keep our herds safe from wild beasts, and take in exchange milk and cheese. We have weapons to use not against other people, but in our own defense, if it's ever required—but that's never happened yet. For those who might want to attack us, we function both as fighters and as prizes for the fight. But not too many men are eager for this kind of prize. The Athenian Solon talked to you about these very same issues, advising you to consider the end. He wasn't talking about present circumstances, but he wanted you to pay more attention to how you could end your life well. He didn't say this outright, since he isn't a Scythian. But if you think it's a good idea, pass on my advice to Cyrus and all the other tyrants, since it will be more useful for those still in power than for those who've already been ruined.

10. Anacharsis to Croesus

I've come, king of Lydia, to the land of the Greeks in order to learn their customs and habits. I don't need gold; it's enough for me to return to Scythia a better man. That's why I've come to Sardis, hoping to make your acquaintance.

Apollonius

Letters 1–4, 6–8: Apollonius to Euphrates

1. From Apollonius to Euphrates

I'm friendly towards philosophers, but I'm not at all friendly at the moment (and may I never be in the future!) towards sophists, teachers, or other such wretches. Don't take this personally, unless you're one of them; but I do mean you personally when I say the following: control your emotions, try to be a philosopher, and don't be jealous of those who really are philosophers, since you're already on the doorstep of old age and death.

2. *To the same person*

Virtue comes from a person's natural quality, from learning, and from habit; so each of these approaches to virtue just mentioned might be worth considering. Do you think you might try one of these options? Either stop playing the sophist from this point on, or give your teachings away as a gift to those who happen to pass by, since you're already as rich as Megabyxus.

3. *To the same person*

You've traveled between Italy and Syria, your native country, strutting around in so-called "royal attire." You used to have just a simple cloak and a long white beard, nothing more. So why are you returning now from this sea voyage, bringing a cargo full of silver, gold, all sorts of merchandise, fancy clothes, and other accessories, including vanity, trickery, and evil intentions? What kind of cargo is this, and what kind of strange new commerce? The great philosopher Zeno only traded in dried fruit.

4. *To the same person*

Your children don't need much if their father is a philosopher. You shouldn't worry about acquiring more than the basics, especially since it would come together with a bad reputation. But since it's happened, the second step would be to hand out some of your possessions to other people right away. You have, after all, both a fatherland and friends.

6. *To the same person*

I asked some rich men if they were unhappy, and they answered, "How couldn't we be?" Then I asked them the reason for their distress, and they blamed their wealth. But you, poor man, are just recently wealthy.

7. *To the same person*

If you reach Aegae and unload your ship there, you must return to Italy as soon as possible and kiss up to everyone: sick people, old men, old women, orphans, the wealthy, the enfeebled, any slave named Midas or Getas. They say that the trader has to let out all his sails, but I'd rather wear out my saltshaker in a house that honors Justice.

8. *To the same person*

Would you, too, like to indict me? If only you had the guts! Then you'd list these standard easy objections: "Apollonius totally refuses to take a bath." Yes, but he never leaves his house, so his feet stay clean. "No one ever sees his body move." That's because his soul is always moving. "He lets his hair grow long." Yes, and so do Greek men, because they're Greek and not barbarian. "He wears linen clothes." That's because linen is the purest fabric for holy men. "He practices divination." Yes, since many things are unknown, and there's no other way to predict the future. "But such activity isn't appropriate for a philosopher." Yet it is appropriate for a god? "He cures physical pain and stops suffering." Well I guess the same complaint could just as easily be brought against Asclepius. "He eats alone." While other men stuff themselves. "His words are few and quickly spoken." Because he can't be totally silent. "He avoids all meat and animal flesh." That makes him human. Euphrates, if you say you've already brought these accusations against me, maybe you can add this: "If he'd been able, he would've taken cash, gifts, and citizenship papers, just as I did." No, if he'd been able, he wouldn't have. "But he might have accepted gifts for the sake of his fatherland." You can't call it a "fatherland" if it doesn't understand what it possesses.

Demosthenes

Letter 4

Demosthenes sends greetings to the Council and the Assembly [of Athens]. I've heard that Theramenes [a rival politician] has been slandering me, saying that I bring bad luck. I'm not surprised that he doesn't realize that verbal abuse neither damages the person against whom it's spoken nor influences decent men. It would be even odder if he did understand some of this, given that his lifestyle is violent, he's not a citizen by birth, and he was raised from infancy in a whorehouse. If I ever return home safely, I'll try to talk to him about the drunken insults he hurls at both of us, and even if he has no shame, I think I can make him a bit more self-controlled. But for the sake of our common advantage, I want to let you know by letter what I have to say about this. Pay attention and listen, because I think my words are not only worth hearing but also worth remembering.

I believe your city is the luckiest of all and the most beloved by the gods, and I know that Zeus at Dodona, [the goddess] Dione, and Pythian Apollo always affirm this in their oracles, testifying further that you have good fortune in your city. As far as good fortune is concerned, the gods turn to prophecy for the future but base their assessment of the past on past events. The things I've done as a citizen in Athens belong to the past, and contributed to the gods' calling you fortunate. So how can it be fair for those who followed my advice to be called fortunate, while I myself, who gave the advice, receive the opposite label? Maybe someone might argue that my advice for the common good was really the gods' doing, and they don't lie; but that the slander Theramenes directed against me was personal. I would say he must have been a rash, shameless, and stupid man to argue that way.

It's not just the oracles of the gods that will prove your good luck, but also a clear look at the events themselves, if you collect all the facts properly. If you're willing to inspect the events from a human perspective, you'll discover that the city, thanks to my advice, has been very fortunate. But if you think you deserve to receive the blessings that the gods alone receive, you're aiming for the impossible. What is it that's reserved for the gods but unavailable to men? Just this: to be in complete control of all the good things in the world; to have them yourself and give them to others; never in all your life to experience anything bad or anticipate such an experience. Now that I've clarified this, the next step is to compare your fortune with that of the rest of the world. Nobody would be stupid enough to claim that what's happened to the Spartans (whom I never advised) or the Persians (I've never even set foot there) is preferable to your current situation. I don't need to mention the Cappadocians, Syrians, and the men who live in India, at the ends of the earth; all these men have suffered many truly terrible experiences. Everyone will agree, by Zeus, that you're better off than these, yet worse off than the Thessalians, Argives, and Arcadians, or any other of those who fought on Philip's side. But I think things have turned out much better for you still, for two reasons. First, you weren't enslaved (what can match that?), and second, those allies are blamed for all the bad things that have happened to the Greeks because of Philip and their enslavement, and so they're hated with good reason; in contrast, you're perceived as having fought hard for the Greeks, risking your life, property, city, land, and everything else. As a reward, all civilized men should grant you glory and eternal gratitude. In sum, because I advised you, your city has fared best of all those that resisted Philip, and it's even ended up with a better reputation than those cities that allied themselves with him.

Therefore, while the gods give you good oracles, they turn the unjustified slander back on the head of the speaker. Anyone would understand the situation if he chose to examine the way that man lives; he prefers to do the very things that someone might slander him for! He hates his parents but loves that prostitute Pausanias; he's as bold as a man, but lets himself be penetrated like a woman; he acts better than his father, but is really the lowest of the low. He delights in things that disgust everyone else—filthy language and stories that offend his audience—but he keeps on talking as if he were a nice guy with nothing to hide. I wouldn't have written this if I hadn't wanted to remind you of his faults. Each one of you, reminded by my words, knows how many terrible evils can be attributed to this man, evils a decent man would hesitate to utter or even to write down, and would certainly be disgusted to hear about. So you can agree that I've said nothing shameful, and whenever this man shows his face, he's a reminder to everyone of his own evil nature. Farewell.

Diogenes

Letters 6, 22

6. To Crates

After you left on your trip to Thebes, I was walking up from Piraeus in the middle of the day when I became terribly thirsty. I rushed over to the well of Panope, and while I was taking my cup out of my bag, someone ran up—it was one of the fieldworkers' servants—cupped his hands together, dipped them in the well, and drank. I thought this was a much smarter way to drink than using a cup, so I wasn't ashamed to accept him as a teacher of good habits. I threw away my cup, and since I found some people going in the direction of Thebes, I'm sending along a letter for you with this pearl of wisdom. I don't want to learn anything good without sharing it with you.

You should come to the market too, where many people spend their time. Then we can discover even more interesting things about humanity, one at a time. Nature is great, but since appearance has pushed Nature aside, our job is to restore Nature and thus save humanity.

22. To Agesilaus

Life is so uncertain that I'm not even sure I'll still be alive when I finish writing you this letter. But my bag has all the treasures I need for living. What the honored gods provide us with is greater than men think. One thing I do know for sure: first we're born and then we die. Since I know this, I banish the vain hopes that flit around my poor body, and I advise you not to think more deeply than a mere mortal should.

Hippocrates and Democritus

Letters 10, 11, 18, 20

10. From the Council and the people of Abdera to Hippocrates, greetings

The greatest danger currently threatens our city, Hippocrates. One of our citizens, someone we always expected would bring fame to the city both now and in days to come (and let's pray the gods won't begrudge it now with this situation), has been infected by the weight of wisdom that oppresses him. And if Democritus [the philosopher] has lost his mind, we're afraid that our city of Abdera will be totally abandoned. He used to ignore everything, including himself, but now he stays awake day and night, laughs at everything large and small, and his philosophy is that life in general isn't worth a thing. One man gets married, another occupies himself with imports and exports; one man is active in politics, and another governs, is an ambassador, votes, becomes sick, is wounded, dies. But Democritus laughs at all of it, whether he sees men depressed and gloomy or cheerful. The man studies things in Hades and writes about them; he claims the air is full of phantoms, and he listens to the voices

113

of birds. He often gets up at night, alone, and seems to be singing softly. He says that sometimes he wanders off into space and that there are countless Democrituses just like him there. His face is as disfigured as his reasoning.

This is what's troubling and confusing us, Hippocrates. Come quickly, save us, and advise our country. If you save him, you'll gain fame, money, and an even better reputation for learning. And we know that you care a lot more for learning than for good fortune. But you'll get a lot of the latter from us too, ungrudgingly, since we're talking about Democritus' life here. Even if it's a question of gold, the city won't fall short in any way of your expectations for reimbursement. Our lifestyle has become infected, Hippocrates, or gone crazy. You're the best of men—come and cure our most prominent citizen, not as a doctor, but as the founder of all Ionia, building a sacred protective wall around us. You'll heal the whole city, not just a man; you'll make it possible to reopen a diseased Council that's in danger of closing down. You'll come yourself as lawgiver, judge, ruler, savior, and craftsman of these things. This is what we expect, Hippocrates, and we hope you can do it all for us. It's not just any old city at stake; all of Greece needs you to protect the embodiment of wisdom. The goddess of learning herself seems to come to you as an ambassador, begging to be released from this insanity. Wisdom is something everyone is born with, but some people like you have an even greater share. You should know that future generations will rejoice if Democritus fully attains the truth he hopes for. You're involved with Asclepius both through family ties and through your occupation; Asclepius is also a nephew of Heracles, who in turn is an ancestor of Abderus, who is, as you surely know, the person our city is named after. So curing Democritus would be a favor to him, too. You can see, Hippocrates, how our people and this famous man are wasting away into nothingness—we beg you to hurry up and come to us. It's unfair how even abundant good luck can become an illness. Democritus was strong enough to scale the heights of wisdom, but now he's equally in danger of being ruined by insanity or just plain silliness. All the other Abderites, the ones who remain uneducated, keep their common sense, but since they were foolish before, they're now less foolish about judging the wise man's disease. You should come with father Asclepius; come with Heracles' daughter Epione; come with her sons who fought at Troy; come right now and bring Apollo's cures for disease. May your land produce roots, plants, and medicinal flowers that prevent and cure insanity. Let's hope that the land and the mountain peaks will never be more fruitful than right now, growing healing plants for Democritus. Farewell.

11. *From Hippocrates to the Council and people of Abdera, greetings*

Your fellow citizen Amelesagoras came to Cos on the day of the Assumption of the Staff, which, as you know, is an annual holiday for us; the festival includes a fancy parade to the cypress grove, usually led by people related to the god. But since Amelesagoras' words and attitude seemed to suggest something serious, I was convinced that his business was urgent (which it was). I read your letter and was amazed that the whole city, like a single man, was in total confusion over a single man. Blessed are the people who know that their best defenses aren't towers and walls, but good men, and the wise minds of wise men. I'm convinced that human science is a gift from the gods and that men are works of Nature; don't be angry with me, men of Abdera, if I say that it isn't you men, but Nature herself who calls me to rescue her creation which is in danger of collapsing from its disease. So instead of obeying you, I'm now obeying Nature and the gods by healing Democritus' disease, if it really is a disease and you haven't made a bad mistake—I pray that's the case. It's even greater evidence of your goodwill that you were upset just by a small suspicion of trouble. But neither Nature nor god would promise me money for coming, so you men of Abdera shouldn't force me to take money, but rather let me practice the free tasks of my free science. Men who accept money force their knowledge into slavery, trading their previous freedom of speech for complete servility. The result is that they might lie, saying a disease is more serious than it is, or claiming it's nothing, just a small infection; they might promise to come but not show up, or again show up uninvited. Human life is a pitiful thing, since an intolerable love of money has permeated the whole of it, like a wintry wind. If only all the doctors would come together to cure a sickness worse than madness; instead, men think money is a blessing, even though it's really an evil disease. I think all disorders of the mind are forms f madness, which introduces certain extreme beliefs and fantasies in the intellect; the man who is cleansed of them through virtue becomes healthy again. If I wanted to become rich by any means, men of Abdera, I wouldn't come to you for the sake of a mere ten talents; no, I'd be visiting the great king of Persia, where whole cities are loaded down with wealth acquired by men. I would be curing the plague there, if I hadn't refused to liberate a country hated by Greece from the horrible plague; in my own way, I can also fight a naval battle against the barbarians. I would have been disgraced if I'd accepted money from the king and luxuries offensive to my native land; if I had flaunted such luxuries, I would've been seen as the destroyer of Greek cities. You can't make money any way you want. Justice lives in the great shrines of virtue: these shrines aren't hidden, but clear for all to see. Don't you think it's just as bad to save one's enemies and to save one's friends for pay? That's not the way I behave, people. I won't profit from disease, nor did I pray to hear about Democritus' insanity. If he's healthy, he'll be my friend; if he's sick, he'll be an even better friend once he's cured. I've heard that he's a serious man with a solid character, and your city's pride and joy. Farewell.

18. From Democritus to Hippocrates, I hope you're well

You came to me thinking I was crazy, and planning to dose me with hellebore; you'd been convinced by foolish men who thought my work was madness. Actually at the time, I happened to be writing about the order of the cosmos, the orbit of the stars and the heavens. Since you know the nature of these things, how very precisely they're designed, and how far removed they are from madness and insanity, you praised my nature and decided those boorish men were the crazy ones. There are many things that move across the sky changing their appearances to confuse us, things that are seen in the cosmos with shifting forms; my mind has examined the nature of all these things and brought them clearly into the light. And if you want proof, read the books I've written on the subject. Hippocrates, you shouldn't have met and associated with such men, since their minds are superficial and weak. If you'd been convinced that I was mad and given me the drink, that drink would have really driven me out of my mind, and they would have blamed your medical science as a contributing cause of my insanity. If you give hellebore to a healthy person it clouds the mind, while it usually brings relief to someone who's gone mad. Think about this. What if you'd found me not writing, but lying down, or walking around deep in thought, talking to myself, alternating between being frustrated and smiling at my own cogitations, but not paying any attention to my acquaintance's conversations, obsessed with my own thoughts and intense investigations? You would've thought that Democritus, judging by what

116

you could see in front of your eyes, was the very image of insanity. But a good doctor should diagnose a condition not by appearance alone; he should determine the disposition as best he can from a person's actions, whether the condition is just beginning, at its peak, or coming to an end. He should closely observe the case's specifics, the season, the person's age, while treating the condition and the whole body. It's from all these things that you'll easily find the root of the disease. I've enclosed my treatise on insanity for you to read. Farewell.

20. From Hippocrates to Democritus, I hope you're well

Most men, Democritus, don't praise a doctor's successful skill, but instead they often attribute a cure to the gods. But if nature works against things somehow and gradually weakens the patient, then the same men blame the doctor and ignore the gods. It seems to me that medical knowledge gets more blame than respect. I haven't yet learned everything about medicine, even though I'm already quite old, and neither did the discipline's founder, Asclepius, but he, too, changed his mind about things many times, as the books written about him by others have shown us. The letter you sent me criticized the idea of using hellebore medicinally. I was called to give you hellebore, Democritus, because you were thought to be mad, but I hadn't figured out what sort of person you were. When I met you, I realized, by Zeus, that this wasn't a case of losing one's mind, but of intense mindfulness. So I eagerly praised your nature and judged you the best interpreter of Nature and the cosmos; then I blamed those who had brought me there and labeled them madmen. They were the ones who needed medicine, not you. Since it was chance that brought us together, the best thing would be for you to write to me often and share with me any books you've written. I've enclosed my treatise on hellebore for you to read. Farewell.

Isocrates

Letter 7: To Timotheus

I'm sure you've often heard about the friendship between our families. I'm delighted to hear that you're managing your present position of power better and more sensibly than your father Clearchus did, and that you've chosen to acquire a good reputation instead of great wealth. Your decision is a sign not of moderate virtue, but of the highest possible kind. So if you stick to your plan, you'll soon be surrounded by men who'll be eager to praise your good attitude and wise choices. And I think the rumors about your father will add more credibility to the public's opinion that you have good intentions and are better than the others. Most people usually praise and honor sons of cruel or harsh fathers more than those of honorable ones, as long as the sons seem nothing like their fathers. It's much more pleasing if something good occurs in spite of all expectations to the contrary, rather than just predictably.

So keep this in mind, and start planning how you can correct the problems of the city, turn its citizens towards good works and self-control, and make them live more happily and optimistically than in the past; think about choosing some friends and advisors. These are the duties of a smart and honest ruler. There will always be some men, however, who'll scorn such duties, caring only to live their lives in wild extravagance, abusing and overtaxing their best, richest, and smartest citizens. These men just don't understand that intelligent men in positions of power shouldn't focus on their own pleasure at the expense of others, but should take great care to make their citizens happier; they shouldn't ignore their own safety while acting harshly and cruelly towards all others. No, their behavior should be so polite and proper that nobody would dare plot against them, yet at the same time they should carefully protect their bodies as if there were an assassin at every corner. If they adopted this plan, they'd be out of danger and honored by all men, and it's hard to imagine a better situation than that. I've been thinking while writing this letter how well everything has turned out for you. Your father has left you great wealth, which could only have been acquired through force, tyrannical behavior, and at the price of great hatred; now it's up to you to use it well for the good of the people, so make sure you handle it carefully.

That's my two-cents' worth, and here's how it works. If you crave possessions, more power, and the dangers involved in acquiring these things, you'd better send for different advisors. If you're satisfied with your material possessions but crave virtue, a good reputation, and the goodwill of your people, pay attention to my advice, imitate those who rule their cities well, and try to do even better.

I've heard that Cleommis, the ruler of Methymna, is good, noble, and wise in all he does. Instead of killing any of his citizens, exiling them, confiscating their property, or harming them in any other way, he offers complete security to his fellow-citizens, brings back the exiles, gives back to those who return whatever property they have lost, and promises a full refund to those who purchased the property. On top of that, he gives weapons to all the citizens, assuming that nobody would try to attempt violence against him; if anybody should dare, he thinks it would be better to die after having treated the citizens so virtuously, rather than to live longer and become the cause of the worst evil for the city.

I would have said more about these things, and maybe even said it more elegantly, if I didn't have to write this letter so quickly. So I'll give you more advice later, if my old age doesn't stop me, but for now I'll explain my own business. Autocrator, the man bringing this letter, is a friend of mine; we share the same vision about things, and I've often benefited from his skill. I've given him advice about visiting you. For all these reasons I want you to take good advantage of him, in a way that will help both of us; and make sure he knows he's benefiting from my recommendations. Now don't be surprised that I'm so eager to write to you, since I never asked your father Clearchus for anything. You see, just about everyone sailing here from Heraclea says that you are like the best of my associates. As for Clearchus, all those who met him when he visited here agreed that back then he was the most liberal, kind, and generous of my associates. But when he took power, he seemed to change so much that everyone who knew him before was shocked. That's the reason I became estranged from him. But I think well of you, and I'd value your friendship. You'll prove to me soon whether you return my feelings by taking good care of Autocrator and sending me a letter reaffirming the friendly relations we had before. Farewell, and if you need anything from me, don't hesitate to write.

Plato

Letter 13

Plato sends greetings to Dionysius, tyrant of Syracuse.

Let the words above function both as the first line of my letter and at the same time as a sign that it is from me. Once when you were hosting some young men from Locria at a feast, and you were sitting at some distance from me, you approached in a cheerful mood and said something that struck me, and the person sitting next to me, as quite clever. My dining companion, one of the beautiful young men, then responded: "Dionysius, you must find Plato invaluable when it comes to intellectual matters!" And you answered: "He is invaluable in many other ways too, since from the moment I invited him here, I benefited greatly just from the very fact of inviting him." Let's keep up our good relationship so that we can continue to benefit mutually from one another.

In order to promote this, I'm now sending you some reading material: parts of the Pythagorean writings and the *Divisions*, as well as a man (we discussed this earlier) whom you and [the Pythagorean philosopher] Archytas might find interesting, if indeed Archytas has come to your court. The man's name is Helicon, and he was born at Cyzicus; he studied with [the famous astronomer] Eudoxus and is well trained in all his teacher's doctrines. He's also spent time with one of Isocrates' students, as well as with Polyxenus, [the mathematician] Bryson's friend. Furthermore, unlike most philosophers, he's quite charming when you meet him, not at all stuffy; on the contrary, he seems pleasant and easy-going. Of course I say all this with some hesitation, since I'm just giving my opinion about a man, and men in general, while not totally worthless, are certainly unreliable creatures in most ways. So even in the case of this man, I was concerned enough after meeting him to observe him closely for a while myself, and suspicious enough to question his fellow citizens about him; but nobody had anything negative to say. You can observe him yourself, but do it discreetly. If you have any spare time, I think the best thing would be for you to take lessons from him in addition to your regular philosophy studies; but if you don't have the time right now, ask him to instruct someone else, who can in turn teach you when you have the leisure to learn. That way you can become a better person with a nobler reputation, and the benefit you obtain from me won't ever be lost. Enough said on that topic.

You wrote asking me to send you some things. I purchased the statue of Apollo, which Leptines is bringing to you, from a young but talented artist named Leochares [a student of the famous sculptor Scopas]. There was another statue at his shop that I thought was very well done. I bought it intending to give it to your wife [the niece of Dion], since she took such good care of me while I was sick and while I was well, in a manner that reflected well on both of us. So please give it to her, unless, of course, you think it's not a good idea. I'm also sending twelve jars of sweet wine and two jars of honey for the children. We arrived too late to buy any dried figs, and the myrtle berry preserves turned out to have spoiled; next time we'll have to be more careful. Leptines will tell you about the plants.

I obtained the money for all this, i.e. the items mentioned above, as well as for some unpaid city taxes, from Leptines. I told him what seemed the most honorable thing for us to say, which also happens to be the truth: that the amount we paid for the Leucadian ship—the sum of about sixteen minas—should be refunded to us. That was the sum I received; I spent it myself, and then sent you the items.

Now I should tell you how your accounts are doing, both your own funds at Athens and what you've given me. I will use your money, as I've already told you, in the same way as I use that of my other friends: I spend as little as possible, just as much as my benefactor and I think necessary, fair, or appropriate. This is how things stand at the moment. Around the time when you ordered me to wear a crown, but I refused, my nieces died, leaving their four daughters in my care. One is old enough to be married, another eight years old, another just over three, and the last one not quite one. My friends and I feel obligated to give them dowries, as long as I am still alive to see them married; if not, they'll have to fend for themselves. Actually, I don't feel obligated to the girls whose fathers may become wealthier than I am, even if right now I'm the richest; after all, I'm the one, along with Dion and some other friends, who gave their mothers their dowries. Now the oldest daughter is getting married to Speusippus, her uncle. I don't need to give her more than thirty minas—that's a reasonable dowry from us. In addition, when my mother dies, I won't need more than ten minas to erect her tomb. So at present, these are my basic needs and anticipated expenses. If I incur any further expense, whether private or public, because of my visit to Syracuse, I'll stick to my earlier promise to try to spend as little as possible; but if I can't make payments, I'm sure you will cover the costs.

The next thing I want to discuss is how your own money at Athens is being spent. First, if I have to pay for a chorus or some other large project, you should know that not a single friend of yours is willing to contribute anything, as we had first thought; second, if you yourself need a large sum of money, it would be much better for your reputation to have it immediately available, rather than having to wait for a messenger to arrive with it, since such a situation is harmful to your good name and is even a mark of dishonor. I found this out myself when I wanted to send you some other valuable items you'd asked for in your letter. I sent Erastus to Andromedes, the one from Aegina who's your friend, because you'd told me I could borrow from him whatever I needed. Well, he said, not surprisingly, that once before he'd lent you money from your father's account, but that he'd had a very hard time getting you to pay it back; so now he wouldn't give you more than a very small amount of cash. That's why I had to borrow the money from Leptines, who is really worth his weight in gold, not just because he gave you the loan, but because he gave it eagerly, and showed in many other ways, through his words and his actions, what a good friend he is. I think it's my duty to report such things to you, whether good or bad; you should know what people think of you.

And now I'll tell you the truth about your accounts. It's the right thing to do, and on top of that, I have an insider's view of your court. Your regular messengers don't want to bring you petitions they think include demands for payments; they are worried that they'll be blamed for it. You should get them used to the idea that they must report these messages as well as the others. It is very important that you understand the whole picture as best you can; you must assess the situation clearly and not hide your head in the sand. This is the best way to protect your power. You've always insisted on this point, and I'm sure you will continue to insist upon it: that to spend your money wisely while paying back loans in a timely fashion is the best way to do business and make even more money. So don't let those men who pretend to be your friends say vicious things behind your back. It isn't at all good for your reputation to be considered a difficult person to do business with.

My next task is to talk to you about Dion. I can't speak about certain other matters until your letters arrive, as you mentioned already. I obviously didn't say a word about the news that you told me I couldn't share with him. But I did try to find out whether he would react well or badly to the idea [perhaps of giving up his wife Arete to a court favorite; Plutarch *Dion* 21], and I suspect that if you do carry through with your plan, he will take it very badly indeed. Still, as far as everything else is concerned, Dion seems to be on your side, both in word and deed.

Let's agree to give a foot-soldier's breastplate made of soft material to my friend Cratinus, Timotheus' brother, and three dresses of seven cubits' length to Cebes' daughters; make sure they're sewn from Sicilian linen, not from that expensive fabric from Amorgos. You probably recognize the name of Cebes. His name appears in the Socratic works, along with Simmias, conversing with Socrates in the dialogue on the soul [the *Phaedo*]; he's a well-meaning and good friend to all of us.

I'm sure you remember the secret sign that marks which of my letters are serious and which are not, but pay attention anyway and read carefully. Lots of people ask me to write them letters, and I can't easily or publicly refuse them all. So the word "god" appears in the beginning of a serious letter, while the word "gods" appears in a less serious one [—oddly, neither appears in the beginning of this letter]. The ambassadors, appropriately, also asked me to write to you. They eagerly sing our praises everywhere they go, especially Philagrus, in spite of his injured hand. Philaides, too, was talking about you, when he returned from visiting the Great King in Persia, and if I were in the mood to write a really long letter, I would write down what he said; but now you can find out from Leptines.

If you decide to send me the breastplate or any of the other things I've listed, give it to a man you trust; if you don't have a courier available, you can give it to Terillus, who is one of those men who's always about to sail off somewhere. He's a friend of ours, and well informed in many areas, including philosophy. He's Tison's son-in-law, who was a civic magistrate in Athens when we set off on our voyage.

I wish you well, and urge you to study philosophy and to encourage the other young men to do the same. Greet your comrades for me, the ones who enjoy contemplating the celestial spheres. Tell Aristocritus and the others that, if a message or letter addressed to you arrives from me, they should make sure you know about it as soon as possible, as well as reminding you to pay close attention to its contents. Also, don't forget to repay your debt to Leptines; pay it back as quickly as you can so that other people, seeing how prompt you are with him, will be even more eager to be on our side.

Iatrocles, now my freedman, is sailing along with Myronides, and will bring the things I'm sending you. Please give him a position with a salary in your household; he thinks well of you, and you can use him for any job you have in mind. Finally, keep this letter, either the document itself or a summary of its contents in your own words, and above all, be true to yourself.

Socrates and the Socratics

Socrates Letter 6

I took care of the two visitors, as you asked me to do, and I found one of our associates who will speak to the people on their behalf. He said he was happy to help because he wants to do you a favor too. Now let me respond to your questions about profit and the things you teased me about in your letter. I suppose it's not surprising that some people want to know, first, why I've chosen a life of poverty while others chase eagerly after wealth; and second, why, when I could receive a lot of money from a lot of people, I intentionally refuse gifts not just from friends who are still alive, but also from friends who've died and left things behind for me. It's no wonder that other men think I'm crazy, acting like this. But you need to take into account not just this bit of information, but also the other parts of our life, and if we seem different in the way we treat our bodies, don't be surprised if we also have different views on the issue of money. I'm perfectly content to eat the simplest food, and to wear the same clothes in both summer and winter; I don't need shoes at all. I don't want political fame beyond what I get from being wise and just. But those who live extravagantly don't deprive themselves of anything in their lifestyle: they change clothes not just once a year but every day, and they indulge in illicit pleasures. In the same way, those with bad complexions beautify themselves with cosmetics, and those who have lost the honest reputation of virtue (which every man should have) find refuge in a reputation based on flattery, as they bribe the crowd through free food and public entertainments. I think that's why such people are so needy: because they can't live on a small income, and others don't want to flatter them without being paid for their compliments. As far as I'm concerned, my life is just fine in both ways, and if I'm wrong about something, I'm the first to admit it. I know full well that the best sort of people and the masses disagree on what's better for mankind. And often when I wonder why god is happy and blessed, I realize that he's better than we are because he needs nothing. It's a mark of a splendid nature not to need much and to be ready to enjoy life. It makes sense that the person who imitates the wisest man is himself quite wise, and the person who makes himself most like a happy man is himself the happiest. If wealth could do this, he would have chosen wealth. But since virtue alone seems to produce this, it's silly to abandon true goodness and pursue the appearance of goodness. Nobody could easily persuade me that I'm not better off this way.

But about the question of my children and what you said about needing to provide for them, I'm happy to make my views about them public. In my opinion, proper thinking is the one true source of happiness. The man who has no brains but trusts in the value of silver and gold first believes he's acquired something good that he doesn't really have, and then becomes much more miserable than other men. One person who struggles in poverty will come to his senses sooner or later, while another person, thinking he knows what it means to be happy, ignores what's really useful, is spoiled by his affluence, and fails to obtain something truly good for mankind; and on top of that he's deprived of any hope of anything good in the future. It's impossible for such a man to arrive safely at a state of virtue, since he's held back by the flattery of men who hang around him; he's seduced by pleasures that attack the soul through all the senses and sneakily drive out any goodness or moderation that might be in it. Why would I want to leave behind for my children a source of foolishness rather than education? Haven't we shown them through both words and actions that they have to take responsibility for themselves? If they don't become good there's no point in living; they'll die pitifully, ravaged by insatiable hunger, paying a penalty that fits their crime of laziness. And yet the law insists that children should be raised by their parents until adulthood. But perhaps some citizen, irritated at his sons for coveting their inheritance, might say the following:

> Are you planning to bother me after I'm dead? Will the living ask the dead for food? Aren't you ashamed to live your life less actively than a corpse? Why do you think my funds will be more than enough for others after my death when yours aren't enough even for you to live on now?

Thus he might speak somewhat awkwardly to his sons, combining a father's authority with civic free speech. My resources may be rather modest when it comes to words, but in terms of action I'm closer to wealthy men. So I won't leave behind gold for my sons; I'll leave them a possession more valuable than gold, namely good friends. If my sons retain the friendships, they'll have all they need, but if they treat their friends badly, it will be clear that they would have handled money even worse.

If you think I've made the wrong decision, based on what you've seen of other people's negligence, think about it this way. First, not all men treat their friends the same way; some men provide for their friends even after they're dead. Second, our friends are quite special, not like the common lot, and we'll treat them well now and in the future. So it's clear that a small favor earns in exchange small compensation, but long-term good deeds engender compensation appropriate to the benefit. I predict my own deeds will seem better to my friends in time to come. That's why I'm not demanding payment from them, because I can't think of an appropriate compensation for philosophy except friendship, and because I'm not concerned about material things, as are the sophists. They grow more intelligent as they age, and people think more highly of them because they're old; that's why students in particular love them, and revere the father who begat them. He's esteemed while alive and his memory is honored after his death. If he leaves behind a family member, they care for him as if he were a son or a brother, showing him every consideration, since they're connected to him not by family ties but by something else. So even if they are tempted to, they can't neglect him when he's sick, just as we can't ignore our blood relatives. The kinship of the soul is like a brother born of the same father; it compels people to help a dead man's son, reminding them of his father, and if they neglect him, it reflects badly on their honor.

So now tell me if you still think I'm handling my affairs badly or neglecting my children, so that when I die they won't lack the basic necessities of life. I'm not leaving them any money, but rather friends who will be financially responsible and personally involved in their care. Nobody to this day could ever say that he's become a better man because of money. A genuine friend is a better choice than genuine gold: he doesn't support everyone who begs for help, but only his best friends; he doesn't pay attention just to life's bare necessities, but also to his friend's soul; and most of all he's living proof of the argument for virtue, without which human life would be useless. We will explore these things more precisely when we meet in person; I hope I've answered your questions sufficiently now in my brief response.

Socratics Letter 21

From Aeschines to Xanthippe, wife of Socrates

I gave Euphron of Megara six dry quarts of barley for you, the sum of eight drachmas, and a new coat to help you through the winter. Please accept these gifts. I'm sure you know that Eucleides and Terpsion are both good, honest men who have the best intentions towards you and Socrates. If the children ever want to come to visit us, don't discourage them, since Megara isn't so far away. It's enough, my dear, that you've cried so many tears already; crying won't help, and it might even hurt you. Remember what Socrates used to say and try to follow his habits and advice, since grieving all the time won't do you or the children any good. I like to think of them as Socrates' baby birds: we must try to feed them and also stay alive ourselves for them. Because if you or I or someone else who cares about the children of Socrates (may he rest in peace) should die, they'll be the ones to suffer, without anyone to help raise them. So try to stay alive for their sake. But you can't do this without providing for your own basic needs. Grief seems to stand in opposition to life, since the living are harmed by it. Apollodorus (the so-called "madman") and Dion sing your praises because you don't take handouts from anyone but still claim to be rich. You're doing the right thing there, because as long as I and your other friends are able to help you, you'll have everything you need. So cheer up, Xanthippe, and don't reject any of Socrates' good ideas, since you know what a great man we think he was. Focus on how he lived and how he died. I think that even his death was great and good, if one examines it in the right way. Farewell.

"Letters of the seven sages": Solon and Thales

Solon (Diogenes Laertius 1.64–7)

1. Solon to Periander

You've sent me a message that many people are plotting against you. Act quickly now if you want to get rid of them all. Someone you don't suspect at all might start scheming—someone who's afraid for his own skin, or prejudiced against you because you're such a complete coward. Whoever found out that you weren't suspicious would earn the city's gratitude. The best way for you to avoid being blamed is to quit right now. But if you're determined to be tyrant, think about making your hired thugs more powerful than the city's defense force. Then no one can harm you anymore and you won't have to get rid of anyone.

2. Solon to Epimenides

So it turns out that my laws didn't help the Athenians much, nor did your purifications of the city. Religion and laws alone can't help cities; but men who lead the masses any way they want can make a difference. So as long as things are going well, religion and laws are useful; but if things are going badly, they're useless.

All my law-making didn't do much good either. Those in charge undermined the public good and couldn't dislodge Pisistratus from his tyranny. Nobody believed me when I predicted the worst. The Athenians trusted that flatterer more than me when I told the truth.

I threw my weapons down at the general's doorstep and announced that I was smarter than those who couldn't see that Pisistratus wanted to be tyrant, and braver than those who hesitated to confront him. Then they decided Solon was mad. Finally I protested: "My country, this is Solon speaking, ready to protect you in word and deed. Some Athenians think I'm crazy, so I'll leave them, the odd man out who hates Pisistratus. Let them go and be his bodyguard, if that's what they want." As I'm sure you know, my friend, that man was dead set on being tyrant. He started out as a popular leader; then he took a knife and cut himself, went off to Athens' supreme court claiming he'd been attacked by his enemies, and demanded a personal guard of 400 young men. The people who wouldn't listen to me did listen to him, and they gave him the men, who were armed with clubs. After that he destroyed the democracy. My attempts to free the poor people of Athens from their servitude were in vain, since now they're all Pisistratus' slaves.

3. Solon to Pisistratus

I'm confident you won't hurt me. Before you became tyrant, I was your friend, and now I have nothing more to argue about with you than any other Athenian who's not fond of tyranny. Let each man decide for himself whether it's better to be ruled by one man or by a democracy. I'm willing to admit that you're a fantastic tyrant. But I also see that this isn't a good time for me to return to Athens. Since I granted the Athenians equal civil rights and refused at the time to become tyrant myself, who wouldn't blame me if now I returned and accepted everything you're doing?

4. Solon to Croesus

I'm delighted by your kindness toward me, and by Athena, if I weren't so set on living in a democracy, I'd rather have settled in your kingdom than here in Athens, where the tyrant Pisistratus rules in violence. But I prefer to live where equal rights belong to all. I will come to visit you for a while, though, since I'm eager to be your guest.

Thales (Diogenes Laertius 1.43–4)

1. Thales to Pherecydes

I hear that you're planning to be the first Ionian to enlighten the Greeks about theology. Maybe you made the right decision to publish your treatise openly rather than handing it over to a particular person, which wouldn't have been a good idea. But if the idea appeals to you, I'd love to chat with you about what you've written; just let me know, and I'll join you in Syrus. Solon the Athenian and I have already sailed to Crete to study there, and then we sailed to Egypt to spend time with holy men and astronomers, so we'd be crazy now not to do the same for you. Solon will come too, if you like. Meanwhile you are such a homebody that you rarely come to Ionia, nor do you have any desire to see strangers. Instead, I suspect you spend all your time doing one thing, namely writing, as opposed to Solon and me; we never write anything and travel all over Greece and Asia.

2. *Thales to Solon*

If you ever leave Athens, I think you could very easily settle in Miletus with our colonists. You'll find no danger here. But if it bothers you that we Milesians are ruled by a tyrant, since you hate all forms of absolute power, at least you might enjoy spending time with your friends. Bias wrote to invite you to Priene. If the city of Priene appeals to you more, go live there and we'll join you too.

6

INVENTED
CORRESPONDENCES,
IMAGINARY VOICES

INTRODUCTION

Three major authors are associated with independent collections
of invented correspondences in the period of the Second Sophistic:
Aelian, Alciphron, and **Philostratus.** All three choose epistolary
form as a medium for displaying short scenes of emotional intensity,
or to invent predicaments in the personal lives of others. The impetus
for their compositions, as in the case of the authors in earlier chapters,
can be traced back to the rhetorical characterizations (*ethopoieia*) so
popular at the time. Their compositions reveal little or no character
development, sustained plot, or dramatic rhythm; instead, these
writers use the letter as a kind of justification for a brief glimpse
into the lives of (mostly) ordinary people. The letters are portraits,
as it were, as opposed to moving pictures, soliloquies rather than
dialogues. They present one side of an issue and usually leave the
matter unresolved, open to multiple resolutions in the mind of
the reader.

Aelian's and Alciphron's collections of fictional letters make up a
whole fourth-century BCE Athenian world in miniature, but a world
that seems deliberately to exclude the educated elite, in deference to
the uneducated and socially inferior. Parasites and courtesans become
representatives of the great cultural heritage of classical Athens, in a
kind of witty paradox that elite readers of the Second Sophistic must
have enjoyed (Davidson 1997; Anderson 1993: 183–5). Fishermen
and farmers boast of their own particular kind of *paideia* (Aelian *Letter
20*), as do their urban counterparts. This leads to such contests of
wisdom as Alciphron's debate between a courtesan and a philosopher
as to who is the best teacher of men (Alciphron *Letter 4.7*), or, to cite
a contemporary, Lucian's comparison between Odysseus and Plato in
his paradoxical treatise in praise of parasites (*De Parasito*).

The *Farmers' Letters* are attributed to **Claudius Aelianus,** a Roman author who also wrote two works of paradoxography: *De Natura Animalium* and *Varia Historia.* Scholars have suggested that Aelian may have been a younger or less talented contemporary of Alciphron, particularly since Aelian's anthology shrinks Alciphron's four diverse epistolary categories down to one, writing only in the voices of farmers (Benner and Fobes 1949: 345). But it is equally possible that Aelian did not directly imitate Alciphron's work, and that both authors were inspired by earlier sources, particularly comedy (Bonner 1909). Whatever the nature of his inspiration, the farmers' letters are well worth reading.

Aelian's twenty letters are transmitted under the heading "from the rustic letters of Aelian"; this phrasing may suggest that the surviving texts are merely a selection from a larger collection (De Stefani 1901). The individual letters each reflect the perspective of its imagined writer; they are rustic vignettes, small slices of country life, unified by their setting and the stereotypical nature of their characters. Each letter has a named sender and addressee, sometimes borrowed from comedy (e.g. *Letters 13–16:* Callipides to Cnemon), at other times imaginary speaking names (e.g. *Letter 1:* Euthycomides [Straight-hair] to Blepaeus [Sharp-eyes]). The collection includes two sets of paired letters (*Letters 7–8, 11–12*) and one group of four (*Letters 13–16*). These sets of grouped, answered letters satisfy the reader's interest in a slightly more sustained conversation, while the single, unanswered letters from writers who appear only once in the corpus offer the reader fresh topics of interest. The first type of organization resembles Alciphron's interrelated courtesans' letters in his fourth book (*Letters 4.1–5*), while the latter functions as an apparently arbitrary mélange of country letters presented in the name of entertainment.

Aelian displays his literary skills by imagining what farmers might write to one another. This scenario required an imaginative leap for his elite audience, as most farmers were not literate, and even if they were, they would certainly not be capable of writing allusive, sophisticated prose. Aelian's choice also demanded a careful balance in terms of the letters' contents, as the sordid reality of most country life clashed with a more idealized literary vision of a golden age of innocence and plenty. Aelian responded to the challenge in two ways. First, he stayed true to his subject by including enough down-on-the-farm talk about harvesting, beekeeping, border disputes, disease, and petty theft to satisfy the reader's curiosity about "common folk," while interspersing amusing references to events and characters familiar from the comic stage, such as love affairs, greedy courtesans, wild youths, and grumpy old men. Second, he confronted the paradox of clever rustics head on in the last letter of the collection, which concludes (*Letter 20*):

> If you think these letters sent to you are too clever for the countryside to produce, don't act so surprised. We're not from Libyan or Lydian backwaters; we are Athenian farmers.

Our reaction to the final line is a combination of knowing disbelief and admiration for the author's brash justification for his own sophistic product.

The translations below represent both paired and individual letters. In *Letters 7* and *8*, a young farmer falls in love with the courtesan Opora (the name means "Ripe for plucking") and sends figs, grapes, and wine in an attempt to seduce her. She, of course, wants only cash, and answers him with the conventional comparison between a woman's body and ripe fruit to explain her need to get rich while she is still young and attractive. *Letter 10* is a joke from one farmer to another: if your son runs around too much, try castrating him; what works for goats should work for men as well. Farm logic is thus extended to its logical extreme. *Letters 13* and *14* are the first two in the group of four exchanges between the farmer Callipedes and his neighbor Cnemon, the stock misanthrope familiar from Menander's play *Dyscolus* or Lucian's dialogue *Timon*, both of which may have directly inspired Aelian (Costa 2001: 126; Rosenmeyer 2001: 315–17). Callipedes' letter of friendly advice is met with an outpouring of verbal abuse, and at the end of the exchange, the situation remains unresolved. The final selection is *Letter 18*, where we meet a farmer who has abandoned his farm in the hopes of striking it rich as a marine merchant. His friend who stays behind expresses the conventional wisdom that, even if farming is a hard life, at least it is relatively safe—less prone to capsize, at any rate (cf. Alciphron *Letters 1.3*; *2.4*).

Farmers reappear in the pages of **Alciphron**, whose collection of one hundred and twenty-three fictional prose letters is organized into books under the four headings of farmers, fishermen, parasites, and courtesans (Bowie 1985: 679–80; Benner and Fobes 1949). Little is known about Alciphron's life (ca. 170–220 CE), because he is never mentioned by name in antiquity (Ussher 1987; Reardon 1971: 180–5). A few of the letters in the collection include conventional epistolary openings and closings; most resemble short essays or narrative descriptions with no acknowledgment of their epistolary framework. All, however, share their inclusion of an internal audience, a character directly addressed whose existence justifies the necessity of a written letter.

In some manuscripts, Alciphron is called *rhetor* and "Atticist," labels that also fit his contemporaries Aelian and Philostratus (Swain 1996: 17–64). In his discussion of the Second Sophistic, E.L. Bowie claims that "the archaism of language and style known as Atticism is only part of a wider tendency, a tendency that prevails in literature not only in style but also in choice of theme and treatment" (Bowie 1970: 3–4). Thus Alciphron turns his eye to fourth-century BCE Athens: his style is atticizing, and his themes are borrowed from such popular Athenian authors as Demosthenes and Menander, to name just two. He evokes both a rural (farmers, fishermen) and an urban (parasites, courtesans) environment, and balances the varied perspectives of individual voices by combining them into a kind of common record of daily life among the lower classes. The cumulative effect of the collection is that of a busy canvas illustrating a segment of society and culture long gone (Gratwick 1979; Reardon 1971: 182).

The mundane topics of Alciphron's letters and their characters' sharp observations of differences between socio-economic classes are traits borrowed from New Comedy, with its interest in impoverished young women and clever parasites. Alciphron's people live in circumscribed conditions but write of their longing to break out of their assigned places: fishermen envy the stability of farmers, parasites want to strike it rich, country girls aspire to city living. Their dreams are more often than not thwarted. In the entire collection, the only successful move upward on the social and economic scale belongs to Menander, who is invited to Egypt by the king; yet he hesitates to accept the invitation, reluctant to abandon his girlfriend for fame and riches. The letters thus uphold and to some extent celebrate the stability of social order, just as most comedy does, while allowing the reader the temporary pleasure of grumbling along with the writers about the temptations and disappointments of human life.

If a Menandrian muse stood at one shoulder, Alciphron's former schoolteacher, whoever he was, must have stood at the other. Alciphron's adaptation of *ethopoieia* to epistolary form transformed the humble school exercise into a high literary art. His letters start from the premise of what a particular person might say in a stressful or surprising situation, but it is his individual presentation of speaker and situation that shows his real skill. Alciphron succeeds in creating believable portraits by trying to see things through each character's eyes, even though most of his invented characters evolve from comedy's stock in trade. This is not to say that we necessarily feel empathy or compassion for these characters. Alciphron does not give us the impression that he has actually spent time with a farmer, for example, or come away with a feeling of respect or sympathy for the working classes. On the contrary he seems to tailor his portraits to the tastes of the more sophisticated reader, ourselves included, who has a superficial and maybe even a pointedly unsympathetic view of such types. For the most part, we are invited to laugh at his creations, not with them.

Thus we inevitably enjoy our superiority in *Letter 2.28*, included in this volume, when a farmer, aptly named Philocomus ("Village-lover"), feels uncomfortable uttering the word "city," since in his rustic naiveté he has no idea what "that thing is," and finds it hard to imagine many men living all together behind one wall. In *Letter 1.11–12*, also included below, we read a letter exchange between a girl in love and her mother, married to a fisherman. As the girl Glaucippe ("Sea-green") praises the beauty of her boyfriend from the city, her vocabulary betrays her: "his hair is curlier than seaweed, his smile more radiant than a calm sea, and the sparkle of his eyes is like the dark blue of the ocean . . ." (1.11.2). Just as the farmer can't utter the word "city" without discomfort, so the girl can't escape the language of her upbringing. Her mother responds caustically that her father will sooner feed her to the fishes than see her move to the city, effectively deflating Glaucippe's romantic urban fantasies and reminding her of her place in the world. Yet Alciphron hints that our young heroine is more sophisticated than we first think: she quotes Sappho (or perhaps Menander's version of Sappho, in his play *Leucadia*), threatening to follow in her steps and commit suicide for the sake of love.

The sheer variety of Alciphron's epistolary *ethopoieiai* is astounding. The experiences range from the mundane (*Letter 2.3*: farmer requests a loan of wheat) to the pornographic (*Letters 4.13* and *14*: rustic orgies). Most of the characters are wholly invented, with grandilo-quent "speaking names": the parasites in particular have the lion's share of humorous names, and in the selections below we meet, among others, Stemphylochaeron ("Hail to the olive paste") and Trapezocharon ("Devourer of the dinner table"), Conoposphrantes ("Whiff of gnat") and Ischnolimus ("Lean and hungry"). Only the last book, the letters of the courtesans, differs from the rest of the corpus in that it fictionalizes the voices of famous historical lovers such as the sculptor Praxiteles and his beloved Phryne (4.1), the philosopher Epicurus and his Leontium (4.17), or the playwright Menander and his Glycera (4.2, 18, 19).

My selection below attempts to do justice to this varied and complex collection. I have chosen half a dozen letters from each of the four books, highlighting some of Alciphron's main topics: the hardships of poverty, the poor man's envy of the rich, the universal prejudice against philosophers, paternal admonitions, moralizing tirades, the troubles of parasites and courtesans at the hands of their patrons, and, cutting thematically through all four books, the difficult consequences of falling in love.

Finally, we come to the seventy-three love letters (*epistolai erotikai*) by **Philostratus of Lemnos**. Although four known family members can lay claim to that name, the most likely author of these love letters is Flavius Philostratus II (ca. 170–240 CE), who studied rhetoric in Athens and later moved to Rome, where he came under the patronage of the emperor Septimius Severus and his wife, Julia Domna (Bowersock 1985: 95–8; Anderson 1986: 274–5). Two other works are commonly attributed to this Philostratus: the *Lives of the Sophists*, and the *Life of Apollonius of Tyana*.

The seventy-three letters differ greatly from one another in length and topic, and, in spite of the collection's title, are by no means all "erotic." At one end of the spectrum is the one-line aphorism of *Letter 65*, to Epictetus ("Fear the people with whom you share great power"); at the other is the lengthy *Letter 73*, addressed to the empress Julia Domna, in which Philostratus explores at length the relationship between Plato, Gorgias, and other famous sophists, and discusses contemporary cultural trends while advising his patroness on matters of literary taste. There are also letters of advice, recommendation, and business, as well as letters accompanying gifts. But by far the largest number of letters is addressed to unnamed beloved boys and women, alternately praising and blaming, confessing love and complaining of neglect, all variations on the theme of erotic persuasion.

Scholars have traditionally divided the collection into two main groups, both written in Philostratus' own voice, but addressed to different recipients and arranged according to subject (Benner and Fobes 1949: 394–402; Kayser 1871). There are fifty-three erotic letters in the first group: twenty-three addressed to unnamed boys (1, 3–5, 7–11, 13–19, 24, 27, 46, 56–8, 64), and thirty to unnamed women (2, 6, 12, 20–3, 28–39, 47, 50, 54–5, 59–63). The second group is a miscellany of twenty letters (40–5, 48–9, 51–3,

65–73): two are erotic (48, 53, both "to a certain friend"); eighteen deal with a number of different subjects and are all addressed to named persons. The classification of "erotic" does not do justice to Philostratus' stylistic range, as the love letter often includes a variety of other literary devices or narrative styles, such as mythological allusions, catalogues and lists, and paradoxical *encomia* (praise of something intrinsically unworthy of praise). Philostratus' collection, like those of Alciphron and Aelian, functions as an exercise in sophistic variation. But he differs from these two authors in that he presents himself as the letter writer rather than assuming an invented persona (cf. Trapp 2003: 33). We are invited to imagine the author himself in love, ostensibly sharing his own experiences with us in the letters, and the focus on the author is further intensified by the mostly anonymous identities of his addressees. As a result of Philostratus' use of the first person, the reader is affected differently than was the case with the third person narratives of Alciphron, for example. While we don't go so far as to imagine these letters as true confessions, we are likely to feel more sympathetic and less superior to this particular author in love.

Philostratus depicts letter writing as the lover's obsessive occupation, and his own letters are written with the goal of winning his beloved. Against our better judgment, on one level the letters feel to us as if they were actually sent to their addressees. But Philostratus frequently writes with such rhetorical flourishes and elaborate allusions (e.g. to Homer, Plato) that it is difficult to read his lines as anything other than literary showpieces. This is true particularly in the letters of erotic persuasion, where Philostratus takes one theme and plays with it in half a dozen letters to different addressees. He argues that promiscuity is evil (*Letters 22–3, 27, 40*), but then gleefully argues just the opposite elsewhere (*Letters 19, 38*), going so far as to say that it is precisely the beloved's status as prostitute that appeals to him. In a letter translated below, Philostratus praises the new growth of a boy's beard (*Letter 15*), but then later advises his beloved to use any means possible—shaving, plucking, depilatory creams, drugs—to restore his smooth skin (*Letter 58*). What are we to think: that Philostratus is a versatile writer, a fickle lover, or both? Philostratus adjusts his opinions like a wily politician, and he shifts addressees in order, it seems, to increase the odds that he will get lucky, thus characterizing himself as an undiscriminating and even unscrupulous lover. But this only comes out if we read the collection as a whole; if we imagine the impact of a single letter on a single recipient, we can imagine it comes across as quite sincere.

Philostratus' letters reflect sophistic training more overtly than Aelian's and Alciphron's, again perhaps because he presents his unmediated voice as writer; choosing not to create variation in assumed voices, he injects it into his own. His voice is not only constantly shifting, but also highly idiosyncratic in its erotic attitudes, and a streak of masochism runs through the collection. The author presents himself as a victim of *eros*, and his letters deal with this victimization by alternately begging, threatening, persuading, praising, scolding, and commanding. His sophism also reveals itself in word play: while most of Philostratus' letters ignore formal epistolary convention, *Letter 14* assumes familiarity with basic epistolary etiquette and then subverts it:

> I send you greetings (*chaire*), even though you don't want them, greetings (*chaire*), even though you don't write back . . .

Reminiscent of a similar device in Rufinus' Hellenistic epigram discussed earlier, the repetition of *chaire* puns on the courtesy inherent in the conventional letter opening ("Greetings from x to y") while contrasting the writer's eagerness with the boy's neglect: he will return neither love nor letter to his admirer.

The eight letters selected below highlight some of Philostratus' recurring themes. I have already mentioned his clever manipulation of epistolary convention (*Letter 14*), his opinions about male puberty (*Letter 15*), and his convenient acceptance of a beloved's promiscuity (*Letter 19*). *Letter 7* may be modeled on Socrates' arguments in Plato's *Phaedrus* for the "best" kind of lover; it expounds the advantages of an impoverished lover over a rich one, just as elsewhere he argues paradoxically for the advantages of a foreign lover over a citizen. *Letter 11* includes some of his favorite erotic clichés: the eyes as the site of erotic power, military and hunting metaphors for love, and love experienced as a burning flame. *Letter 55* reflects his frequent use of rose imagery. *Letter 22* tries to convince his beloved that she needs no adornment, particularly cosmetics. This theme reappears with a twist in several letters to both boys and women, recommending total nakedness as the ideal state of the beloved; barring that, the object of his affection should at least walk barefoot. Philostratus indulges further in the theme of bare feet in *Letter 37*, where he begs permission to kiss his beloved's toes and to be stepped on by the beloved's beautiful foot. Elsewhere, in letters not included here, he begs to be tortured, maimed (*Letters 5, 47*), and killed (*Letters* 7, 23, 57), all in the name of love. Most of the letters in the collection may reveal more about Philostratus' supposed personal tastes (as he chooses to present them to us) and less about his social and cultural environment. When we do get glimpses of his society, we need to separate out literary convention from historical reference; thus, the parasite and cook of *Letter* 7 may suggest a fourth-century BCE Greek literary construct inspired by Menander, for example, while the brief reference to Rome in *Letter* 55 has appropriately been used as evidence for placing its author in the second century CE.

As stated earlier, the three authors presented in this final chapter are rarely read by classicists, in spite of their convenient packaging over half a century ago in a single Loeb volume. Most readers, when faced with the multiplicity of Philostratus' and Alciphron's imagined voices, would find themselves either irritated or simply overwhelmed by the artificiality of the genre. Philostratus in particular can be accused of a kind of epistolary "graphomania" more familiar from Choderlos de Laclos' characters in his novel *Dangerous Liaisons*. But the artificiality that bothers us today was a mark of sophism and brilliance for contemporary Greek readers. It is our job to find a way to appreciate these texts on their own, sophistic terms. I hope my selections and translations, in both this chapter and the preceding ones, have assisted my readers in this occasionally daunting yet ultimately rewarding task.

INVENTED CORRESPONDENCES, IMAGINARY VOICES: THE TEXTS

Aelian

Letters of farmers

7. *Dercyllus to Opora*

I won't sing your praises just because you claim you're beautiful and have lots of lovers. They probably worship your body, but I love your name [*Opora* = ripe summer fruit]; I praise you and my family farm in the same breath. I admire the man who cleverly named you Opora, clearly expecting not only city slickers but also country boys to rave about you. So if I've "harvested" Opora, what's wrong with that? Your name is a love tease for everyone, including a fellow who makes a living by farming. I've just sent you some figs from the field, in honor of your name, and grapes and new wine from the vats; in the spring I'll send roses, too, harvested from my meadows.

8. *Opora to Dercyllus*

I suppose you know best whether you're serious about my name or just joking, but I don't think what you've sent me is worth making such a fuss about. Your gifts certainly aren't impressive: two cents' worth of fruit and a vinegary wine that's barely fermented. My slave Phrygia can drink that stuff; I drink fine wines from Lesbos and Thasos, and anyway, I want money. Sending ripe fruit to Opora is like adding flames to the fire. And I think it's better that you know right now exactly what I mean. My name is a good enough reason for me to make money from men who want to be with me, since it teaches me that the body's beauty is similar to a fruit's: when it's ripe, it's fine to take whatever profit you can get for it, but when it droops, I'll turn into a bare bush without fruit or leaves. Nature lets bushes bloom again, but there's only one summer season [*opora*] for a working girl. That's why we need to store up supplies for our old age.

10. *Phileriphus to Simylus*

I've heard that your son is oversexed. So why don't you just grab him and castrate him, the way we do with our goats? It makes the animals calm down and behave much better. And I'm really good at the job: right away I make the animals healthy again, applying salt compresses and pitch plasters. Afterwards your son will be as healthy as a horse and plump as a pumpkin; he'll give up on love affairs and stop wasting your money. You're crazy to keep an uncastrated lover-boy.

13. *Callipedes to Cnemon*

There are lots of good things about life in the country, especially a farmer's gentle temper. Peace and quiet, along with spending one's time tending the land, produce a lovely calmness. But you're wild (I don't know why), a terrible tenant for your neighbors. You hit us with dirtballs and wild pears, and when you see anyone you shriek out loud as if you were chasing a wolf; you're a real problem, you are. If I weren't farming land inherited from my father, I would've given it away already, just to escape this terrifying neighbor of mine. Come on Cnemon, old buddy, change your bad attitude, don't let your temper put you in a rage, or before you realize it, you might really go crazy. Take this friendly advice from your friend; it's medicine for your mind.

14. Cnemon to Callipedes

I didn't really want to answer you, but since you're such a busybody, forcing me to talk to you even if I don't want to, at least it helps that I can contact you through messengers, not in person. So here's your answer—short but not sweet, in what they call the Scythian style. I'm mad, ready to kill, and I hate the whole human race. That's why I throw dirtballs and rocks at anyone who walks by my farm. I think Perseus was really lucky on two counts: he was winged so he didn't bump into people, and was too high up to greet or welcome anyone. I also envy him his amazing ability to turn people into stone. If only I were lucky enough to have that talent, there'd be no shortage of petrified statues, and you'd be the first one I'd practice on. Why do you think you can train me, why are you so eager to make me seem gentle when I hate everyone? That's why, in case you didn't notice, I left the piece of land near the road untouched, and why this bit of earth is without crops. But now you pretend to be one of my buddies, and you're thrilled to have me as a friend, even though I'm my own worst enemy. Why did I ever think it was a good idea to be human?

18. Demylus to Blepsias

My neighbor Laches has quit his job as a farmer, hopped on a boat, and is sailing all over the Aegean (so I've heard); he spends his time surveying the open sea, floating on the waves, living a seagull's life, and battling the winds. He passes one headland after another, nosing around for a nice profit, planning on striking it rich; that's why he said goodbye to his little goats and his former life on the farm. He can't endure the miserable, meager livelihood earned from his fields, and he hates his situation. So he fantasizes about Egyptians and Syrians, imagines their bazaars, contemplates compounded interest, and counts out piles of cash; his mind is on fire, burning with the idea of profit from sailing both ways, and he forgets about storms, strong winds, uncertain seas, and unseasonable bad weather. The rest of us may work hard and gain little, but at least dry land is more stable than the sea, and since it's more reliable, it offers us a safer future.

Alciphron

Book 1: Letters of fishermen

1.11 Glaucippe to Charope

I'm going crazy, mother, because I can't stand the idea of marrying that boy from Methymna, the son of the ship's pilot, the one father just announced my engagement to. I've been madly in love ever since I caught sight of a certain boy from the city; he was a branch-carrier in the Oschophoria procession, and I saw him when you let me go to the city to see the festival. He's gorgeous, mother, just gorgeous, and so sweet. His hair is curlier than seaweed, his smile is more charming than calm waters, and his eyes flash brightly, just like the sea when it's lit up at dawn by the sun's first rays. His whole face— well, you might say that the Graces had left their home in Boeotia, bathed themselves in their favorite spring, and were dancing on his cheeks. He must have stolen the roses from Aphrodite's breasts and put them on his lips, because now they bloom there. Let me be with him, or I'll imitate Lesbian Sappho and throw myself into the waves, not from the Leucadian rock, but from the headlands of the Piraeus.

1.12 Charope to Glaucippe

You're right about being crazy, daughter; you really are out of your mind. What you need is a dose of hellebore, and not just the garden variety, but the most potent stuff prepared in Phocian Anticyra. You're supposed to be a good, modest girl, but now you've lost all sense of shame. Hold yourself steady, choose a straight path for yourself, and push that ridiculous idea far from your mind. If your father should learn about this, he won't stop to think about it at all, but will toss you overboard as food for the fishes.

1.16 Auchenius to Armenius

If you can help me out here, then let me know, but don't tell anyone else about my affairs; if you can't help me, then just be as quiet as a mouse. Now I'll tell you what's up with me. Eros has crept into my heart, and refuses to let reason guide me; passion keeps washing away all my sober plans. I don't know why Eros chose me, a poor fisherman, barely making a decent living; but now that he's inside me, he tortures me and won't go away, so I'm burning up just like some rich guy. I used to laugh at those other guys enslaved to passion, but now I'm all passion myself, and I want to get married right away. I think I see Hymenaeus everywhere I look, the god of marriage, son of Terpsichore, the muse of song and dance. The girl I love is the daughter of immigrants from Hermione; I don't know how they found their way to the Piraeus. I don't have any dowry to offer, but if I present myself well, showing what a good fisherman I am, then unless her father's crazy, I think I can prove myself an acceptable choice as a bridegroom.

1.17 Encymon to Halictypus

Seeing an old and tattered net on the beach at Sounium, I was asking people whose it was and why it was lying there, empty and torn. People said that four years ago, it was your net, but that after scraping a submerged rock, its mesh was ripped right down the middle. It stayed there after that, since you didn't want to repair it or take it away, and none of the neighbors wanted to touch it, because it belonged to someone else. Then for a while it belonged neither to them nor to you, its former owner. So I'm asking you for something that isn't really yours, since it's old and rotten. Since you won't even notice losing something you've already given up for lost, please give it to me as a gift. Best wishes to you.

1.18 Halictypus to Encymon

"Your neighbor's eye is hostile and envious," as the proverb says. Why are you so interested in my property? Why do you think that something I don't care about should therefore become your possession? Keep your hands off, don't be so greedy, and don't let your appetite for other people's things push you to ask for unfair favors.

1.19 Encymon to Halictypus

I didn't ask for something you have, but for something you don't have. Since you don't want to give someone else that thing you don't have, keep what you don't have.

1.20 Eusagenus to Limenarchus

I hope that lookout from Lesbos goes to hell. When he saw dark ripples on the water, he shouted out as if he'd sighted a whole school of tuna. And we believed him and spread our dragnet almost around the whole bay. Then we tried to pull it up, and the weight was greater than you'd expect for a load of fish. Our hopes high, we called over some people nearby, promising to let them share the profit, if they would grab hold and help us. Finally, after much struggling, late in the day, we dragged out a gigantic camel, already decomposing and teeming with worms. That was my fishing experience, and I've told you about it not to make you laugh, but to teach you how many different tricks fortune uses to wear me down, unlucky me.

Book 2: Letters of farmers

2.1 Pratinas to Epigonus

At high noon I chose a pine tree situated in a pleasantly breezy spot, and found some shade under it. As I was cooling off nicely, I thought I would try my hand at some music, so I picked up my pipe and ran my mouth over it; a puff of air came from my lips as they skimmed the pipe, and the sweet pastoral song poured out. Then all my goats gathered around me from every direction, enchanted somehow by the sweet harmony, and they stopped nibbling arbutus and asphodel, completely absorbed in the music. In their midst I pretended to be Orpheus, the son of Calliope. I'm happy to send this good news to you, my friend, since I want you to appreciate how musical my herd of goats is.

2.11 Sitalces to Oenopium

If you are your father's son and agree with me, say goodbye to those quacks, the pale ones with no shoes who hang around the Academy and either can't or don't want to do anything useful to earn a living, but instead waste their time meddling with grand theories of the universe. Leave all this turn to your fieldwork, and if you work hard at that, your storage bins will be filled up with grain, your jars will be heavy with wine, and everything you own will be full of good things.

2.13 Phyllis to Thrasonides

If you wanted to be a farmer, Thrasonides, if you were willing to listen to reason and obey your father, you'd be making offerings to the gods: ivy, laurel, myrtle, and all the summer flowers; you'd be bringing to us, your parents, wheat from your own harvest, wine pressed from your own grapes, and a pail full of milk from goats you had milked. But now you reject field and farm; you rejoice instead in a helmet with three crests, and are in love with your shield, like a mercenary from the backwoods. Don't do this, son; come back to us and embrace a life of peace and quiet. A farmer's life is safe and risk-free: no ambushes, no regiments or phalanxes. Soon you'll have to look after us in our old age. Choose this promise of security over your current dangerous lifestyle.

2.14 Chairestratus to Lerium

Lerium, you're an awful woman, and I hope you meet an awful end. You lulled me to sleep with your strong wine and flute songs, and made me late getting back to my friends on the farm who'd sent me out on this errand. They were expecting me back from the city early in the morning, bringing the clay pots that I came here for. But instead this golden boy of yours listened to flutes all night long and slept well into the day. Leave me alone, you horrible woman, and work your wicked wiles on these unfortunate city boys. If you give me any more trouble, I'll make sure you get your just rewards.

2.21 Philopoemen to Moschium

I feel like I'm sheltering a wolf—that damn slave of mine. He pounced on the goats and destroyed every one of them, either selling or slaughtering them. His belly is always full of wine, and he spends the rest of his money on food, feasting to the music of harp and flute; he loves to hang around the perfume shops. In the meantime, the pens are empty, and the goats that used to live there have vanished. For now I'll keep quiet, so that he won't notice what I'm up to and take off—come here, little goats. But if I manage to catch him off guard, I'll chain his dragging feet with solid shackles, and as he waits patiently for his digging assignment, shouldering pick and hoe, he'll forget all about his life of luxury. A bit of suffering will teach him what it means to live an honest and disciplined life in the country.

2.28 Philocomus to Astyllus

I've never been down to town, so I don't really know what this "city" thing is. But I'm very excited to see this new sight, where men live all together behind one wall, and I want to learn all the ways this city differs from the country. So if you find any excuse for another trip to town, please take me with you this time. I think I'm ready to experience something new, now that I'm old enough to start growing a beard. Who would be a better guide to the mysteries of town than you, since you spend most of your time hanging around inside the city gates?

Book 3: Letters of parasites

3.3 Artepithymus to Cnisozomus

Someone please strangle me; you'll see me soon with my neck in a noose. I can't bear the beatings and drunken behavior of my fellow diners—may they rot in hell—nor can I control my miserable greedy belly, which keeps on asking to be filled not with just any kind of food, but with expensive delicacies. My face can't take the constant slapping; I've been beaten so often that I'm close to losing an eye. Damn it all, the evils I have to endure because of this all-consuming and ever-hungry belly! So I've decided to enjoy one last expensive dinner and then spit out the rest of my life. I think a pleasant death is better than a wretched life.

3.10 Stemphylochaerum to Trapezocharon

I've done very well for myself indeed. You might wonder how, my good friend Trapezocharon. I'll just tell you even before you ask me. As you know, the city has been celebrating the festival of the Cureotis. I'd been invited as entertainment for the dinner, and I was busy dancing the *cordax* dance. The other guests started drinking competitively and the contest looked as if it might go on for quite a while, but then the whole group fell asleep; drowsy slumber whisked them all off to dreamland, even the slaves. I started looking around to see if I could steal any silverware. Since it had all been removed when everyone was still sober, and was now safely hidden, I tucked my napkin under my arm and made a run for it, so fast that I lost one of my slippers on the way. Look how fancy the napkin is: fine Egyptian linen, colored with genuine purple dye from Hermione, a very delicate and expensive fabric. If I manage to sell it without trouble, I'll take you and feed you well at the inn-keeper Pithacnium's place. We've often survived the bad behavior of drunken hosts together, and you should be my partner not only in misfortune, but also on this lucky day.

3.28 *Turdosynagus to Ephallocythres*

Crito was foolish and old-fashioned enough to send his son to study with a philosopher; he decided that the harsh old man who never smiles, the Stoic, was the worthiest of the whole bunch to teach his son. He wanted the boy to learn how to split hairs in speech, and to develop a complex argumentative style. The boy modeled himself on his teacher down to the last detail; he became a serious student not of his teacher's lectures, but of his life and habits. He observed that during the day, his teacher was solemn and stern, critical of his young students; but at night, he wrapped an old cloak around his head and crept around the brothels. So he imitated his teacher perfectly. Four days ago he fell madly in love with Acalanthis, a girl from the Potter's Quarter, and he's all on fire. She's a friend of mine and admits she's in love, but she can see that the boy is consumed with desire, so she's holding out, saying that she won't give in to him until I say she should. She pretended that I had the authority to give the orders in this case. Aphrodite of the people, be generous to this darling woman! She's handling the matter like a good friend, not a girlfriend. Since then I've been taken care of splendidly, with presents just pouring in. And if the stream should flow even more abundantly as time goes on, nothing will stop me, once my master has married an heiress, from buying Acalanthis and making her my wife. She's the reason for my living well, so it makes sense for her to share my life.

3.30 *Gymnochairon to Phagodaites*

Did you see what that damned barber did to me, the one down by the roadside? I'm talking about that gossipy chatterbox, the one who puts out mirrors from Brundisium for sale, trains tame crows, and taps out silly songs with his razorblades. When I went there for a shave, he welcomed me with open arms, seated me on a high chair, put a clean linen cloth around me, and ran the razor very gently over my cheeks, scraping off thick clumps of hair. But that's where he started with his tricky mischief. I didn't realize he was shaving just one part of my jaw, not the whole thing, so that my face was left hairy in some spots and smooth in others. Unaware of his trick, I went off, as usual, to Pasion's house, even though he hadn't invited me. But when the guests saw me, they almost died laughing. I had no idea what they were laughing at until one of them came towards me in the middle of the room, took hold of some of my remaining hair, and tugged at it. Very upset, I grabbed a carving knife and hacked the rest off, and now I'm ready to pick up a good-sized stick and smack that idiot around the head. He dared to mistreat me the way my hosts do, just for the fun of it, but he isn't even offering to feed me.

3.38 Conoposphrantes to Ischnolimus

The hopes I had for the young man Polycritus have blown away with the wind. I used to think that, once his father died, he would put a big chunk of his savings to work. I expected him to invite us to feasts and indulge in other luxuries with us, along with some high-class girlfriends, exhausting most of his inheritance that way. But now that his father has passed away, that boy eats just one meal a day, a very late one, when the sun's already starting to set in the west. And his meal is nothing fancy, just bread from the marketplace; when he celebrates a feast day, he might add a relish of figs or olives. So my great expectations have been frustrated, and I don't know what to do anymore. If the person who is supposed to feed you needs feeding himself, what will happen to the one who needs to be fed? If you put a starving man together with another starving man, the damage is double.

Book 4: Letters of courtesans

4.2 Glycera to Bacchis

My Menander has decided to go to Corinth to see the Isthmian Games. I'm not happy about it; you know what it's like to miss your lover, even for a short time. But I don't want to stop him, since he doesn't often travel away from home. Since he's about to visit your city, I know I should send him to your house, but I'm hesitant to do it, even though I'm sure he wants to spend some time with you, and it would be a nice gesture on my part. I know that we are old friends, you and I. But I'm afraid, my dear, not so much of you (your character is nobler than your profession) as I am of him. He's incredibly passionate, and not even the most puritanical person could resist Bacchis. I certainly don't believe the rumor that he took this trip just as much to see you as to see the Isthmian Games. You might blame me for being jealous, my dear, but you'll have to excuse the suspicious nature of a courtesan. I would be really upset if I lost Menander as my lover. Besides, if we start to quarrel, I'll be exposed to nasty abuse on stage by my fellow actors, like Chremes or Pheidylus. But if Menander returns as devoted to me as he was when he left, I'll be eternally grateful to you. Bye for now.

4.3 Bacchis to Hypereides

All of us courtesans are very grateful to you, and each one of us is as pleased as Phryne. The lawsuit that was brought forward by that criminal Euthias was filed against Phryne alone, but there was a risk involved for all of us. If we demand money from our lovers and don't receive it, or if we get generous clients and then are accused of impiety, it would be better for us to abandon this lifestyle and stop getting ourselves and our clients into trouble. But the way things have turned out, we won't have to blame our status as courtesans because Euthias was shown to be a wicked lover; instead, we can be proud of the fact that Hypereides behaved properly and won the case. You deserve many blessings for your kindness. You've rescued an honest courtesan for yourself, and you've made us want to reward you on her behalf. If you would be so kind as to write out the speech you made in Phryne's defense, then we all promise to set up a gold statue of you anywhere you want in Greece.

4.4 Bacchis to Phryne

I was worried about the danger you were in, my dear, but that was nothing compared to my pleasure when you got rid of your awful lover Euthias and found that wonderful Hypereides instead. I think your trial turned out to be a piece of good luck. That courtroom drama has made you famous not just in Athens but all over Greece. Now Euthias will pay a steep fine by being deprived of your company; I think he misbehaved like a jealous lover because he was so angry, and it didn't help matters that he's basically not very smart. You can bet right now that Euthias is more in love with you than Hypereides is. One man obviously wants to spend time with you because you're so grateful for his help in court, and he imagines himself as your beloved, but the other man is furious at the failure of justice. You can expect prayers, supplications, and piles of money from him all over again. Please don't prejudice people against us courtesans, my dear; don't give in to Euthias' prayers and make Hypereides think he made a mistake. And don't believe people when they say that your lawyer wouldn't have won the case if you hadn't ripped your dress open and shown the judges your breasts. It was precisely his wonderful defense speech that provided you with the perfect opportunity to do just that.

4.7 *Thais to Euthydemus*

Ever since you decided to study philosophy, you've become very full of yourself; your eyebrows practically bump your forehead, you're so supercilious. Then, striking the appropriate pose with a little book in your hands, you rush off to the Academy, bypassing my house as if you'd never seen it before. You're crazy, Euthydemus. Don't you know what kind of person that sophist is, the one who looks so solemn and recites those lectures to you? How long do you think he's wanted to have a date with me? And he's madly in love with Herpyllis, Megara's little maid. Well, I never let him come near me before, preferring to sleep with you in my arms than to have all the sophists' gold. But since he seems to be turning you away from my company, I'll admit him and, if you want me to, I'll show you that this misogynistic teacher of yours isn't satisfied with a typical night's pleasures. This is all just silly nonsense; he's taking money from you boys, stupid. Do you think a sophist is a better person than a courtesan? They may differ from one another in their methods of persuasion, but they both have the same goal in mind, namely to make money. We courtesans are better by far because we're more pious. We don't deny the existence of the gods; instead, we believe our lovers when they swear by the gods that they love us. We don't think it's right for men to sleep with their sisters or mothers or even other men's wives. Maybe we seem to you less worthy than the sophists because we don't know where clouds come from or what atoms are made of. But I myself have studied and talked with many of them. Nobody who spends time with a courtesan dreams of plotting against the state and overthrowing the government; instead he guzzles an early morning cup of wine, gets drunk, and then naps until late in the afternoon. We, too, are teachers of young men. I'd ask you to be the judge between Aspasia the courtesan and Socrates the sophist; think about which one taught the better man. You'll see that the statesman Pericles was her student, while the oligarch Critias was his. So abandon this silly and unpleasant pursuit, Euthydemus my love; it's not right for such lovely eyes to be so serious. Come back to your own true love, the way you used to when you returned from the gymnasium, wiping sweat from your body, so we can get a little drunk and work together towards the beautiful goal of pleasure. And I'm going to prove to you now that I'm really wise: the divine powers have alloted us a short life, so don't waste it on riddles and philosophical nonsense. Goodbye.

4.8 Simalion to Petale

If you're convinced the men who keep you company find it funny or think better of you when they see me always hanging around your door, complaining to the slave girls who've been sent with invitations to men more fortunate than I, then it makes sense for you to mistreat me. You should know that even though what I'm doing isn't in my own best interest, very few of your companions would put up with being neglected the way I am now. I thought strong wine would be some consolation for me, that huge amount I chugged two nights ago at Euphronius' house, and that it would keep me from worrying at night. But it turned out to do just the opposite. It re-ignited my desire so that some of the more sympathetic guests pitied me as I wept and wailed, but others just laughed. It's cold comfort I get—and that bit of comfort has already withered—from the garland you grabbed from your hair and threw at me during our silly fight at the party, just to show how much you hated everything I sent you. If behavior like this makes you happy, enjoy my misery, and if you feel like it, tell my story to those who are happier than I am—but they won't be happy for long; soon they'll be hurting just as I am. You'd better pray to Aphrodite that she not punish you for your arrogance. Some other lover might have written a threatening letter full of abuse, but I'm begging you on my knees here. I'm crazy in love with you, Petale. I'm afraid if I get any crazier, I'll follow in the footsteps of one of those men who've been destroyed by lovers' quarrels.

4.9 Petale to Simalion

I wish tears could support a courtesan's household; then I'd be doing splendidly, since I get such an endless supply from you. But right now I need money, clothes, jewelry, and slaves—that's what makes the world go 'round. I don't have family property at Myrrhinus on the Attic coast, or a share in silver mines; no, I depend on my meager fees and presents wrapped up in sighs from my idiotic lovers. I'm sick and tired of being your mistress for this past year. My hair is dry and brittle, since in all that time I didn't receive even a drop of perfumed oil from you, and I'm ashamed to put on these ancient worn-out Tarantine dresses in front of my girlfriends, I swear it.

How do you think I'm going to make a living if I just sit around
with you? Oh, so now you're crying? You'll stop soon enough.
But in my situation, if I don't have a sugar daddy, I'm going to
starve for real. I wonder about those tears of yours—they're not very
convincing. By my lady Aphrodite, you say you're in love, man; you
crave your girlfriend's company and you just can't live without her.
So what's the problem, aren't there any wine cups in your house
you could sell? Can't you pawn some of your mother's gold jewelry
or call in some of your father's loans? Philotis is the lucky one; the
Graces looked upon her with more sympathetic eyes. What a lover
she has, that Menecleides, who gives her presents every day. That's
a better habit than crying. But miserable me, I have a professional
mourner instead of a lover. He sends me garlands and roses more
appropriate for a corpse, and he says he weeps the whole night
through. If you're bringing me a present, come without weeping;
but if you're not, you'll be torturing yourself, not me.

4.18 Menander to Glycera

I swear to you by the Eleusinian goddesses and their mysteries—
those same ones I've sworn by many times before, Glycera, when we
were alone, you and I—that what I'm about to tell you in this letter
has nothing to do with any desire on my part to boast of my accomplishments or to be separated from you. What could possibly please
me if I were apart from you? And what could delight me more than
your love? Your personality and your manners are so charming that
even our extreme old age will seem as enjoyable as youth. Let's be
young together and then grow old together; by the gods, let's even
die together, Glycera, as long as it's arranged that we can die at the
same time, to avoid any jealousy that may accompany the one who
arrives first in Hades if the other one survives to fall in love with
someone else. Surely I won't experience any such thing when you
are dead, for what pleasure could remain for me then?

I wrote this letter to you while recuperating in Piraeus—you know
about my episodes of nervous exhaustion, which my detractors like
to call self-indulgence and over-sensitivity. I'm sending it to you
while you're staying in town for Demeter's festival of the Haloa,
because it's important news. I just received a letter from Ptolemy,
King of Egypt, in which he extends a sincere invitation, acting in a
very kingly fashion, promising me anything on earth, as they say, if
I will only come to him. He's invited Philemon too, and says that
Philemon has received a similar letter. And now Philemon himself

has written to me, showing me his own royal invitation, which is more casual in tone, written in a less elegant style, since, of course, it isn't addressed to the great Menander. Philemon can consider the situation and make up his own mind.

But I won't wait around for advice. Glycera, you have always been and will now be my advisor, my council of the Aereopagus, and my Heliastic supreme court. You are everything to me, by Athena. So I have sent you the king's letter and ask a double favor: read my letter and also the king's. I want you to know how I've decided to answer him. To set off and sail to a kingdom so distant and remote—by the twelve Olympian gods, I can't bear to think of it. In fact, even if Egypt were as close as Aegina here, I would still never consider abandoning my own kingdom and betraying your love, just to end up alone in a great crowd of Egyptians, separated from my Glycera, gazing at that overpopulated wilderness. It's much more pleasant, not to mention less dangerous, to spend my time in your arms rather than in the courts of kings and viceroys, where free speech is dangerous, flattery contemptible, and success never to be trusted. They can keep their fancy Corinthian pottery, their wine goblets, their golden dishes, and all the expensive stuff in their courts that makes others envious; for all that, I wouldn't trade our annual celebration of the wine pitchers, the drama festivals in the early spring, yesterday's conversations, our exercises in the Lyceum, or the sacred philosophers' Academy. I swear by Dionysus that I would rather be crowned with his Bacchic ivy, as long as my Glycera can sit in the theater and watch me, than with Ptolemy's golden crowns. Tell me, where in Egypt will I see an assembly in action or an issue put to the vote? Where will I see a democratic body participating freely in government, or lawgivers crowned with ivy at city festivals? And where will I see the council's enclosure in the Agora, civic elections, and the feast of the Pots? Let's not forget all those other familiar sights in Athens: the city cemetery, marketplace, courthouses, the lovely Acropolis, the holy goddesses, the mysteries, the neighboring island of Salamis, the narrow channel between the mainland and Salamis, the towns of Psyttalia and Marathon, all of Ionia, the Cyclades, and the entire Greek world—all concentrated in Athens.

So, should I let all this go, leaving my Glycera behind too, and travel to Egypt to find gold, silver, and wealth? Who will share my joy in such riches—Glycera, far off on the other side of the seas? Without her presence, won't these riches seem like deprivation? If I hear that she has transferred her loving affection to some other man, won't all my treasures turn to ashes? And when I die, should I take my sorrows with me but leave behind my money as a prize in the center ring for those who are strong enough to abuse me? Is it really such a treat to spend time with Ptolemy and viceroys and other self-important personages, whose friendship is insincere and whose hatred can be downright dangerous? But if Glycera gets mad at me even for a minute—say no more, I grab her and kiss her all over; if she stays mad, I hug her tighter; and if she still sulks, I dissolve into tears. After this display, she can't stand to see me unhappy anymore, and begs for an end to it, since she has no other protection—no troops, bodyguards, or soldiers—for I am everything to her.

I admit it is a grand and marvelous thing to see the beautiful Nile River; but isn't it equally grand to see the Euphrates? And what about the Ister, or some of those other huge rivers: the Thermodon, the Tigris, the Halys, and the Rhine? If I'm supposed to see all the world's rivers, I'll spend my life drowning in duty, without ever having time to admire my Glycera. The Nile, although beautiful, is teeming with wild animals, and its whirlpools are so scary that no one dares set foot in the water. I hope I'm lucky enough to find a small plot and a tombstone in my own country. King Ptolemy, I will always prefer to be crowned with Attic ivy, to praise Dionysus every year at the hearth, to perform the secret rites of the mysteries, and to direct a new play on stage every year, laughing, enjoying myself, competing, afraid of losing but coming out the winner in the end. I'm happy to let Philemon go to Egypt, where he can enjoy my riches along with his own. Philemon has no Glycera, and probably doesn't deserve one. But I miss you, my dear Glycera; when the Haloa festival is over, please have the horses ready and fly over here to me as fast as you can. I can't recall a longer festival, or one less conveniently timed—but Demeter, please don't be offended.

4.19 Glycera to Menander

I quickly read the King's letter that you sent me. By Demeter, whose temple I'm in right now, I was thrilled at the news, Menander; in fact I was so excited that everyone around me couldn't help but notice. My mother was there, as well as one of my sisters, Euphronium, and one of my friends whom you know. She's often had dinner at your house, and you praised her for speaking like a native Athenian, although you seemed almost afraid to compliment her in front of me—don't you remember that time, Menander, when I smiled at you and kissed you even more passionately than usual?

Well, when my girlfriends noticed such happiness flooding my face and sparkling in my eyes, they asked, "Glycera dear, what wonderful thing has happened? You seem to us more cheerful, more beautiful, completely transformed. Your body practically glows, and this radiance suggests good fortune and an answer to your prayers." And I said, "Ptolemy, the King of Egypt, has sent for my Menander, offering half his kingdom if he will come!" I spoke clearly and in a loud voice so that all the women there could hear me. As I spoke, I waved the King's letter in my hands and showed off its royal seal. "But are you glad to be left behind?" they asked. But that's not it at all, Menander. No one will ever convince me, by Demeter and Persephone, not even if the proverbial ox should utter this opinion, that Menander would ever be willing or able to leave his very own Glycera behind in Athens and live alone in Egypt, king among all his treasures. But this at least was clear in the letters that I read: the King had heard about my relationship with you, and wanted to tease you with a kind of gentle Egyptian version of Attic wit, trying to figure out your intentions. So I'm happy about this fact, that news of our love affair has sailed across the sea all the way to the King in Egypt; he is utterly convinced by such rumors that he's asking for the impossible if he wants Athens to come over to him. What is Athens without Menander, and what is Menander without his Glycera? I'm the one who takes care of the masks and arranges the costumes; I stand backstage chewing my fingernails and trembling with anxiety until the theater claps its approval. Only then do I breathe a sigh of relief, by Artemis, and throw my arms around you, hugging the famous author of these plays. So I told my girlfriends that what made me happy at that moment, Menander, was just this: that not only Glycera loves you, but also kings on the other side of the sea, and that your reputation of great skill extends even overseas. Egypt, the Nile river, Proteus' cliffs on the island of Pharos with its lighthouse—all now hang in suspense, wanting to see Menander and hear his characters: money grubbers, lovers, superstitious old men and women, atheists, fathers, sons, slaves, and every other type who has appeared on stage. Well, they can hear his characters, but they won't see Menander unless they come to Glycera's house here in the city, to witness both my happiness and Menander himself, whose fame travels everywhere, but who spends his days and nights in my arms.

But if you do feel some curiosity about the treasures there, or if you just want to see Egypt, that land of wonder with its pyramids, speaking statues, the famous labyrinth, and all the other things which the Egyptians value for their antiquity or their craftsmanship, please, Menander, don't use me as an excuse not to go; and don't give the Athenians an excuse to hate me, since they are already calculating the bins of corn the King will send them if you go. By all the gods, you should go, and take with you good luck, favorable winds, and a clear sky. But I won't be left behind—don't think for a minute that's what I mean, since even if I wanted to stay behind, I couldn't possibly do it. No, instead I'll abandon my mother and sisters and become a sailor, traveling with you. I'm sure I'll be a great sailor; if an oar breaks, or if you get seasick, I can take care of you. If the sea voyage weakens you, I'll comfort you as I escort you to Egypt. I'll be Ariadne without the thread, and you will be not Dionysus, but Dionysus' servant and ambassador. I won't be left behind on Naxos or some other deserted shore, weeping and wailing about your treachery. There's no need for lovers like Theseus or the faithlessness of men long ago; instead, our lovers' world stands secure, whether it's the city, the Piraeus, or Egypt. No spot will be untouched by our love, and even if we live in the desert, our mutual affection will turn that desert into a cozy lovers' nest. Surely you don't lust after money, luxury, or wealth; no, I know you are totally committed to loving me and to writing your plays. But your family, your fatherland, your friends, just about everyone everywhere, you know, wants to acquire more and more: they want to be rich, to make money for themselves. You'll never criticize me for anything, whether a small point or a big one, I'm sure. Long ago you were overcome by love and desire, but now you've added to these emotions the power of good judgment, which I think is more important, Menander, since I'm afraid that passionate love is short lived. Passionate love is intense but also easily destroyed; if you reinforce that love, however, with clear thinking, then the connection is harder to break, since it includes its share of pleasure without being a source of anxiety. But you can make up your own mind about this, since you often think about these things and have so much to teach me.

But even if you won't criticize or blame me, I'm still afraid of those Attic wasps; they'll start to follow me around everywhere, buzzing in my ear, complaining that I've stolen something valuable belonging to the city of Athens. So my dear Menander, please wait, don't send any message back to the King. Think about it some more, hold off until we're together, and in the company of your friends Theophrastus and Epicurus; this may all seem different when you reconsider it with them. Or even better, let's sacrifice and see whether the omens say it's better for us to go off to Egypt or stay here. We'll send someone to Delphi and consult the oracle, since Apollo is the god of our ancestors. Then, whether we go or stay, either way we can blame the gods.

No, I have another good idea; here's what I'll do. I know a certain woman who just arrived from Phrygia and is quite skilled at predicting the future by investigating animal innards, by considering the tension of their tendons at night, and by revealing the will of the gods. And we don't have to believe her every word, but, as they say, we can at least take a good look. I'll send for her. She told me that first she had to perform a purification ritual and then get some animals ready for sacrifice, as well as obtaining pure frankincense, a big chunk of fragrant styrax, moon cakes, and wild chasteberry leaves. I have a feeling you'll arrive from the Piraeus before she does all that. But if not, tell me honestly how much longer you'll have to wait to see your Glycera again, so I can run down to meet you and have all the arrangements made with this Phrygian woman. Are you trying to make me forget the Piraeus, our little country house, the Munychia, so that all our favorite places may slip from memory? But I can't remember everything, by the gods, and neither can you, since now our lives have become completely intertwined. Even if all the kings in the world should write letters to you, I will always be more important to you than any of them, since you are a faithful lover, true to your sacred vows.

So please try for my sake, my beloved, to come quickly to the city, so that even if you change your mind about joining the King, you'll still have your plays ready for performance, especially the ones most appealing to King Ptolemy and his Dionysus (who, as you well know, isn't a god with democratic sympathies): your *Thais*, or *The Hated Man*, or *The Tough Guy*, or *The Litigants*, or *The Girl Who Was Beaten*, or *The Man from Sicyon*, or whichever plays you are currently working on. I would have to be brash and daring indeed to rank Menander's plays—I'm just an amateur. But your wise love has taught me to understand these things too. You're the one who taught me that a smart woman learns quickly from her lovers; love is eager to get things accomplished. By Artemis, I'm embarrassed to seem unworthy of you by not learning quickly. Don't forget, Menander, to prepare the play in which you've written a role for me, so that even if I can't be with you in person, I can still sail with you to Ptolemy as a character. Then the King can see for himself how strong his power is: he forces you to bring your beloved with you in writing while you leave the real thing behind in Athens.

But you won't leave the real thing behind, don't worry. Until you come to me here from the Piraeus, I'll let myself be initiated into the mysteries of learning how to sail or commanding the bow of the ship, so that I can guide the ship as it sails over calm waves, if this seems the better course of action. I pray to all the gods that whatever you decide will work out best for both of us, and that the Phrygian woman will predict a better future than your *Woman Divinely Possessed* did. Farewell.

Philostratus

Love letters

Letter 7: To a boy

You think I'm not worth bothering about because I'm poor. But even Eros himself is naked, and so are the Graces and the stars. And I've seen paintings of Heracles where he's wrapped up in animal skins, usually sleeping on the ground, or Apollo in just a leather thong, throwing the discus, shooting his bow, or running. In contrast, Persian kings live luxuriously, enthroned high off the ground, protecting their piles of gold with a pretence of holiness; but of course that's why they suffered so badly, conquered by the penniless Greeks. Socrates was a beggar, but rich Alcibiades still crawled under his ratty cloak. Poverty isn't a crime, and financial success doesn't relieve anyone of the duty of getting along with his fellow man. Take a look over there at the theater and you'll see that the audience is all poor people; look over there at the courts, where poor people are sitting; look at the battlefields, and you'll see that wealthy men in gold armor abandon their ranks, while we're the best at fighting. So in this matter of beautiful boys, think about the difference between a rich and a poor lover. A rich man is rude to his beloved, thinking he's bought him, but a poor man feels grateful, thinking he's an object of pity. A rich man gloats over his prey, but a poor man stays silent. Then again, the wealthy man attributes his success to the power of his charisma, but the poor man assumes it's all because of his beloved's charity. The rich man sends messengers—a flatterer, a parasite, a cook, or his table staff—but the poor man arrives himself, showing respect by coming in person. The rich man who gives presents is quickly exposed, since their affair becomes common knowledge to the well-informed crowd; neighbors and even passers-by on the road are fully aware of the situation. But the boy who has a poor man as a lover isn't noticed, since the man is discreet in his demands, avoids blurting anything out to strangers, and doesn't want to encourage other more powerful rivals, something that could easily happen; so he doesn't brag about his good fortune, but instead hides it. Do I need to say more? The rich man calls you his beloved, but I call you my savior; he calls you his assistant, I call you my god; he calls you one of his possessions, but you are everything to me. If he falls in love with someone else, he'll act the same way towards him, but the poor man falls in love only once. Who would sit with you when you're sick, or stay awake with you when you can't sleep? Who would follow you to the army camp or throw himself in front of you to stop a speeding arrow? Who is willing to die for you? In all these things, I'm rich.

Letter 11: To a boy

How often have I opened my eyes wide to let you go, just as hunters open their nets to give wild animals a chance to escape? But you stay put, like those wretched squatters who occupy someone else's land and then refuse to budge. Look, once more, just as I've done before, I'm raising my eyelids: fly away now, stop the siege, and go settle in someone else's eyes. You're not listening; you're clinging even closer and moving deep into my soul. What's this new burning feeling? I'm in danger now; I cry out for water but nobody helps me, because the cure for this flame is hard to find, whether you bring water from a spring or a river. The water itself is burned by love.

Letter 14: To a boy

Greetings—even though you don't want them; greetings—even though you don't write back. You are lovely to others, but arrogant towards me. I suspect you aren't created of flesh and other living materials, but rather of steel, stone, and the river Styx. I hope soon you'll grow a beard and sit outside other people's doors. Truly, Eros and Nemesis are swift and fickle gods.

Letter 15: To a boy

Why, my boy, are you pointing at your beard? You're just at the beginning of your charms, not at the end. Even though the best moment of youth, so brief and capricious, is gone, quenched just like a burst of fire, something solid and secure remains. Time can't harm truly beautiful boys; it points to them as proof of this argument, not begrudging them their beauty. Even Homer calls a boy with a new beard the loveliest, that poet who knows how to observe and also how to create something beautiful. And I don't think he would have said it if he himself hadn't first stroked and kissed the beard of a beloved boy. Before your cheeks began to bloom, they were as soft and clear as a woman's; but now that you're getting the first down on your chin, you're more virile and more perfect than before. What's wrong? Do you want to be like a eunuch, whose cheeks are barren and hard like stones? Those wretches are more embarrassed by that sort of cutting than by the other, since they think their castration is hidden, while bare cheeks cast the most visible reproach on their appearance.

Letter 19: To a young male prostitute

You sell your body, but so do mercenaries; you go with anyone who pays, but so do ships' pilots. We drink you up just as we drink from the rivers, and we pluck you as we do the roses. You please your lovers because you stand naked and offer yourself for judgment, something only beauty can do, since explicitness suits it. Don't be ashamed of your willingness, but take pride in being ready for action. Water is there for everyone, fire isn't just for one person's use, the stars are public property, and the sun is a state-sponsored god. Your body is a temple of beauty, those who enter are priests, and men wearing garlands are ambassadors with silver as their tribute. Rule kindly over your subjects: receive their money and also their worship.

Letter 22: To a woman

A woman who beautifies herself is trying to cover up flaws, worried that her blemishes will be spotted. The woman who is naturally beautiful doesn't need anything else, since she's practically perfect on her own. Eyeliner, hair extensions, blush, lipstick, all the cosmetic lotions and the artificial bloom of rouge have been invented to fix problems. But it is the unadorned object that is truly beautiful. So, if you love yourself as you are, then I love you even more, since I think your unselfconsciousness is proof of your trust in your beauty. You don't use face powder, nor do you line up with the women who use cosmetics, but instead you take your place among those who are truly beautiful, like those women who lived long ago, whom Zeus loved in the shape of gold, a bull, water, birds, and huge snakes. But rouge, wax, slinky Tarentine dresses, bracelets in the shape of snakes, and golden ankle chains are the tricks of courtesans like Thais, Aristogora, and Lais.

Letter 37: To a woman

Momus said that he had no reason to blame Aphrodite—and what could he have complained about?—except for one thing that bothered him: her sandal squeaked, was too noisy, and made an irritating sound. If she had walked barefoot, the way she came out of the sea, that bully wouldn't have found a reason for joking and teasing her. I suspect that this is the only reason she didn't get away with her affair with Ares, because Hephaestus learned the whole secret after her sandal slandered her. So this is the moral of the story. But you seem to think more clearly than Aphrodite, since you use your feet as they were originally meant to be used, avoiding Momus' accusations. O bare feet, o liberated beauty, I would call myself three-times happy and blessed, if only you would step on me.

Letter 55: To a woman

Truly roses are the flowers of Eros. They are young and supple, just like Eros himself. Both have golden hair and resemble one another in other ways as well: roses have thorns instead of arrows, red buds instead of torches, and petals instead of feathered wings; neither Eros nor the rose knows time, for the god Time is hostile to the late season of beauty and the staying power of the rose. I once saw flower-carriers running past me in Rome, indicating by their speed the briefness of the flowers' bloom; their running directs us to enjoy flowers quickly. If you hesitate, it's gone. A woman withers along with the roses, if she delays. Don't hesitate, my love; let's play together! We'll crown ourselves with roses, and race along side by side.

BIBLIOGRAPHY

Altman, J.G. (1982) *Epistolarity: Approaches to a Form*, Columbus, Ohio: Ohio State University Press.

Anderson, G. (1986) *Philostratus*, London: Croom Helm.

—— (1993) *The Second Sophistic*, London: Routledge.

Arnott, W.G. (ed. and trans.) (1996) *Menander*, Cambridge, MA: Harvard University Press.

Barrett, W.S. (1964) *Euripides Hippolytus*, Oxford: Oxford University Press.

Benner, A.R. and Fobes, F.H. (1949) *Alciphron, Aelian, and Philostratus: The Letters*, Cambridge, Mass: Harvard University Press.

Bentley, R. (1697) *A Dissertation upon the Epistles of Phalaris, Themistocles, Socrates, Euripides, and Others*, 2nd edn, London: J. Leake for Peter Buck.

Bonner, C. (1909) "On Certain Supposed Literary Relationships," *Classical Philology* 4: 32–44, 276–90.

Bowersock, G.W. (1985) "Philostratus and the Second Sophistic," in P. Easterling and B.M.W. Knox (eds) *Cambridge History of Classical Literature* vol. 1, Cambridge: Cambridge University Press.

Bowie, E.L. (1970) "Greeks and their Past in the Second Sophistic," *Past and Present* 46: 3–41.

—— (1985) "The Greek Novel," in P. Easterling and B.M.W. Knox (eds) *Cambridge History of Classical Literature* vol. 1, Cambridge: Cambridge University Press.

Calame, C. (1993) "Rythme, voix et mémoire de l'écriture en Grèce classique," in R. Pretagostini (ed.) *Tradizione e Innovazione nella cultura greca da Omero all'età ellenistica: Scritti in onero di Bruno Gentili*, Rome: Gruppo editoriale internazionale.

Cortassa, G. (1990) *Le Lettere di Temistocle*, Padua: Editoriale Programma.

Costa, C.D.N. (ed.) (2001) *Greek Fictional Letters: a Selection with Introduction, Translation and Commentary*, Oxford: Oxford University Press.

Davidson, J.N. (1997) *Courtesans and Fishcakes*, London: HarperCollins.

Derrida, J. (1987) *The Post Card: from Socrates to Freud and Beyond*, trans. A. Bass, Chicago: University of Chicago Press.

De Stefani, E.L. (1901) "Per il testo delle epistole di Eliano," *SIFC* 9: 479–88.

Dihle, A. (1994) *Greek and Latin Literature of the Roman Empire*, trans. M. Malzahn, London: Routledge.

Doenges, N.A. (1981) *The Letters of Themistocles*, New York: Arno Press.

Düring, I. (ed. and trans.) (1951) *Chion of Heraclea: A Novel in Letters*, Göteborg: Wettergren & Kerbers.

Garrison, E. (1989) "Suicide Notes in Euripides' *Hippolytus*," in K. Hartigen (ed.) *Text and Presentation*, vol. IX, Landham, MD: University of America Press.

Gauger, J-D. (2000) *Authentizität und Methode*, Hamburg: Verlag Dr. Kovac.

Goldhill, S. (ed.) (2001) *Being Greek under Rome*, Cambridge: Cambridge University Press.

Goldsmith, E. (1989) *Writing the Female Voice: Essays on Epistolary Literature*, Boston, MA: Northeastern University Press.

Gratwick, A.S. (1979) "Sundials, Parasites, and Girls from Boeotia," *CQ* 29: 308–23.

Gulley, N. (1971) "On the Authenticity of the Platonic Epistles," in R. Syme and K. von Fritz (eds) *Pseudepigrapha* I (Entretiens sur l'antiquité classique, Fondation Hardt 18), Geneva: Vandoeuvres.

Hansen, W. (1996) *Phlegon of Tralles' Book of Marvels*, Exeter: University of Exeter Press.

Harris, W.V. (1989) *Ancient Literacy*, Cambridge, MA: Harvard University Press.

Hercher, R. (1873) *Epistolographi Graeci*, Paris: Firmin Didot.

Hinz, Vinko (2001) Nunc Phalaris doctum protulit ecce caput: antike Phalaris-legende und Nachleben der Phalarisbriefe, Munich: K.G. Saur.

Hodkinson, O. (2005, forthcoming) "Novels in the Greek Letter," in V. Rimmel (ed.) *Orality and Representation in the Ancient Novel*, Groningen: Barkhuis.

Holzberg, N. (1994) *Der griechische Briefroman: Gattungstypologie und Textanalyse*, Tübingen: Gunter Narr.

Jones, C.P. (1986) *Culture and Society in Lucian*, Cambridge, MA: Harvard University Press.

Jost, F. (1966) "Le Roman Épistolaire et la Technique Narrative au XVIIIe Siècle," *Comparative Literature Studies*, 3: 397–427.

Kassel, R. and C. Austin (1983) *Poetae Comici Graeci* vol. 2, Berlin: de Gruyter.

Kauffman, L.S. (1986) *Discourses of Desire: Gender, Genre, and Epistolary Fictions*, Ithaca, New York: Cornell University Press.

Kayser, C.L. (ed.) (1871) *Flavii Philostrati Opera II*, Leipzig: Teubner.

Kennedy, G.A. (2003) *Progymnasmata: Greek Textbooks of Prose Composition and Rhetoric*, Atlanta, Georgia: Scholars Press.

Kindstrand, J.F. (1981) *Anacharsis*, Uppsala: Acta Universitatis Upsaliensis.

Konstan, D. and P. Mitsis (1990) "Chion of Heraclea: A Philosophical Novel in Letters," *Apeiron* 23: 257–79.

Koskenniemi, H. (1956) *Studien zur Idee und Phraseologie des griechischen Briefes bis 400 n. Chr*, Helsinki: Acta Ac. Sc. Fennicae 102.

Lacan, J. (1972) "Seminar on the Purloined Letter," trans. J. Mehlman, *Yale French Studies* 48, 38–72.

Lenardon, R. (1978) *The Saga of Themistocles*, London: Thames and Hudson.

Luck, G. (1961) "Brief und Epistel in der Antike," *Das Altertum* 7: 77–84.

Malherbe, A.J. (1977) *The Cynic Epistles*, Missoula, MT: Scholars Press.

—— (1988) *Ancient Epistolary Theorists*, Atlanta, GA: Scholars Press.

Malosse, P-L. (ed.) (2004) *Les Lettres de Chion d'Héraclée*, Salerno: Helios.

Morgan, T. (1998) *Literate Education in the Hellenistic and Roman Worlds*, Cambridge: Cambridge University Press.

Penella, R.J. (1979) *The Letters of Apollonius of Tyana*, Leiden: Brill.

Penwill, J.L. (1978) "The Letters of Themistocles: An Epistolary Novel?" *Antichthon* 12: 83–103.

Podlecki, A.J. (1975) *The Life of Themistocles*, Montreal: McGill-Queen's University Press.

Reardon, B.P. (1971) *Courants littéraires grecs des IIe et IIIe siècles après J.-C.*, Paris: Les Belles Lettres.

—— (1989) *Collected Ancient Greek Novels*, Berkeley, CA: University of California Press.

Reuters, F.H. (1963) *Die Briefe des Anacharsis*, Berlin: Akademie Verlag.

Rosenmeyer, P.A. (1992) *The Poetics of Imitation: Anacreon and the Anacreontic Tradition*, Cambridge: Cambridge University Press.

—— (2001) *Ancient Epistolary Fictions: The Letter in Greek Literature*, Cambridge: Cambridge University Press.

Rowe, C.J. (2003) *Plato*, 2nd edn, London: Bristol Classical Press.

Russell, D.A. (1983) *Greek Declamation*, Cambridge: Cambridge University Press.

Rütten, T. (1992) *Demokrit: lachender Philosoph und sanguinischer Melancholiker*, Leiden: Brill.

Santini, L. (1995) "Tra Filosofi e Parassiti: L'Epistola III 19 di Alcifrone e i modelli Lucianei," *Aetne e Roma* 40: 58–71.

Schmitz, T. (1997) *Bildung und Macht*, Munich: C.H. Beck.

Segal, C. (1986) *Interpreting Greek Tragedy: Myth, Poetry, Text*, Ithaca, NY: Cornell University Press.

—— (1992) "Signs, Magic, and Letters in Euripides' *Hippolytus*," in R. Hexter and D. Selden (eds) *Innovations in Antiquity*, New York: Routledge.

Smith, W.D. (ed. and trans.) (1990) *Hippocrates' Pseudepigraphic Writings*, Leiden: Brill.

Speyer, W. (1971) *Die literarische Fälschung im heidnischen und christlichen Altertum*, Munich: C.H. Beck.

Steiner, D.T. (1994) *The Tyrant's Writ*, Princeton, NJ: Princeton University Press.

Stirewalt, M.L, Jr. (1993) *Studies in Ancient Greek Epistolography*, Atlanta, Georgia: Scholars Press.

Stoneman, R. (1991) *The Greek Alexander Romance*, London: Penguin.

Stowers, S.K. (1986) *Letter Writing in Greco-Roman Antiquity*, Philadelphia, PA: Westminster Press.

Swain, S. (1996) *Hellenism and Empire*, Oxford: Oxford University Press.

Sykutris, J. (1931) "Epistolographie," *RE suppl.* 5: 185–220.

—— (1933) Die Briefe des Sokrates und die Sokratiker. Studien zur Geschichte und Kultur des Altertums, 18, Paderborn: F. Schöningh.

Syme, R. (1972) "Fraud and Imposture," in R. Syme and K. von Fritz (eds) *Pseudepigrapha* I (Entretiens sur l'antiquité classique, Fondation Hardt 18), Geneva: Vandoeuvres.

Thraede, K. (1970) *Grundzüge griechisch-römischer Brieftopik*, Munich: C.H. Beck.

Trapp, M. (ed.) (2003) *Greek and Latin Letters: an Anthology with Translation*, Cambridge: Cambridge University Press.

—— (2005, forthcoming) "Biography in/and Letters," in J. Mossman and B. McGing (eds) *Biographical Limits*, London: University of Wales Press.

Ussher, R.G. (1987) "Love Letter, Novel, Alciphron and 'Chion'," *Hermathena* 143: 99–106.

Walker, A. (1992) "Eros and the Eye in the Love-Letters of Philostratus," *PCPS* 38: 132–48.

Westermann, A. (ed.) (1839) *Paradoxographoi: Scriptores Rerum Mirabilium Graeci*, Braunschweig (repr. 1963, Amsterdam: A.M. Hakkert).

White, J.L. (1986) *Light from Ancient Letters*, Philadelphia, PA: Fortress Press.

Whitmarsh, T. (2001) *Greek Literature and the Roman Empire*, Oxford: Oxford University Press.

Wohl, V. (1998) "Plato avant la lettre: Authenticity in Plato's Epistles," *Ramus* 27: 60–93.

INDEX

165